GERMANY
CONFRONTS
MODERNIZATION

D1607732

943

CIVILIZATION AND SOCIETY

Studies in Social, Economic, and Cultural History

General Editor

Theodore K. Rabb, Princeton University

Consulting Editors

Thomas W. Africa, State University of New York, Binghamton
David J. Herlihy, University of Wisconsin, Madison
David S. Landes, Harvard University
Henry Rosovsky, Harvard University
Stanley J. Stein, Princeton University
Stephan A. Thernstrom, University of California, Los Angeles

GERMANY CONFRONTS MODERNIZATION

German Culture and Society, 1790–1890

ROBERT ANCHOR
University of Southern California

D. C. HEATH AND COMPANY
Lexington, Massachusetts Toronto London

Clothbound edition published by Lexington Books.

Paperbound International Standard Book Number: 0-669-81026-6
Clothbound International Standard Book Number: 0-669-81034-7

Library of Congress Catalog Card Number: 70-179800

PREFACE

This book is not a survey of German history from the French Revolution to the end of the Bismarckian era. Instead, it deals with Germany during that time in terms of its transition from a premodern to a modern society. That transition was not successful, as the Germans consistently failed to effect a rapprochement between continuity and change, between inertia and momentum, between native traditions and borrowings from abroad, and between their own national existence and that of others. For that reason, however, few phases of history offer a richer field for an exploration of the tensions, turmoil, and disruption involved in modernization than the century or so during which Germany emerged from a divided, stagnant, feeble society into a highly centralized, streamlined world power. For Germans were the first major European people, outside of the tiny corner of northwestern Europe where the forces of modernization crystallized, to feel their full impact once modernization entered its expansive phase by way of the French Revolution. The clash of forces that occurred first on German soil foreshadowed similar clashes that have subsequently occurred, *mutatis mutandis,* throughout most of the rest of the world.

Thus, if Germany did not successfully negotiate the transition from a traditionalistic to a modern society, its very failure served to enlarge the picture of what that transition involves. At the very least the German experience showed that there is nothing automatic or natural about modernization. It also raised the question, for the first time on a significant scale, of whether avenues to modernization existed other than the Western one. It raised the question of what the relations between societies at different stages of development can and ought to be and of how a society in transition is to relate to itself and its past. These general problems and pressures, first confronted in their full amplitude by Germany in the nineteenth century, most of the rest of mankind has had to contend with since.

Germany's failure to resolve these problems and tensions had disastrous consequences for itself, for Europe, and for the world. Its failure, however, not only enlarged, but also enriched in some ways the scope of the process of modernization, particularly as regards the role of culture in a changing society. For German cultural and intellectual life during the nineteenth century, especially the first half, was one of the richest and most creative in all of world history. And, as with any great culture, that of Germany did not merely passively reflect its social and historical environment; it also responded to it critically and creatively. In the case of German culture this meant coming to grips with all the intellectual and spiritual problems posed by Germany's development toward the modern. Specifically, it meant filling the void left by Germany's steady rejection of the premises of modern Western thought and civilization; the rejection of Cartesian philosophical premises, natural law theory, constitutional and representative government, utilitarianism, and individualism. It meant also a constant reexamination and reevaluation of the relationship between Germany's past and the effects of rapid innovation in the life of Germany and in Europe as a whole. Above all, it meant a searching inquiry into the function and purpose, the concept and content of culture in modern society, and what the relationship of the artist and philosopher can and ought to be to it.

In short, what sustained German thought and culture at such a high level for a time was its bold critical and creative encounter with the most basic spiritual problem that modernization poses wherever it makes itself felt: the problem of self-redefinition, both on a social and an individual scale. This problem—how it manifested itself in Germany, how it was dealt with there, and what it signified, with respect to German culture in particular and to the development of Western society at large—that is the unifying theme of the present book.

ROBERT ANCHOR

CONTENTS

ILLUSTRATIONS

Part One

FROM REVOLUTION
TO RESTORATION:
1789–1815

Germany? But where is it?
I do not know how to find
the country.

                    Goethe

The French Revolution entered into the life of Europe and the world beyond as a harbinger of the modern, that nebulous, complex constellation of forces which included the rise of the centralized state, the middle classes, capitalism, overseas expansion, nascent industrialization, Newtonian science, utilitarian philosophy, and faith in secular progress. While it is true that all of these developments had originated in the West, it is also true that they had in the main crystallized within a comparatively small area, circumscribed by London, Paris, and Amsterdam. In 1789, therefore, the modern could not be neatly equated with the West or with westernization. Ireland, the Iberian peninsula, and southern Italy were scarcely touched by these developments. On the other hand, such non-Western states as Prussia, Russia, and the Habsburg Empire had been affected by them, at least to some extent. Poland thought, and would continue to think, of itself as a bastion of the West, while Latin America, along with the overseas powers controlling it, has to this day proven more resistant to modernization than some areas of Eastern Europe and Asia.

If the forces of modernism acted as divisive agents in Europe, the forces of tradition, reacting to them, came to function as agents of cohesion. On the eve of the Revolution, before the two directly collided, tradition served to consolidate Europe in the face of the forces that by now threatened to fracture it. The *ancien régime* still prevailed almost everywhere: dynastic politics, a predominantly agrarian economy, a hierarchical social order, a still serious concern with religion—these were the rule rather than the exception. Cultural and intellectual traditions also were still

THE PROBLEM OF SELF-REDEFINITION

international: Classicism, Baroque, and Rococo were as much in evidence in Vienna, Dresden, and Madrid as they were in Rome, London, and Paris. Petersburg was built in the Italian Renaissance style, Moscow thought of itself as a third Rome, Leipzig as a second Paris, Weimar as a second Athens, Vienna as the seat of a universal Catholic empire, and Hamburg and Göttingen as outposts of the enlightened West. Richardson, Rousseau, and Goethe were read and appreciated throughout Europe. What was common to Europeans in the eighteenth century, therefore, was still as significant as what was working to divide them.

In 1789, then, the West was no more a well-defined, monolithic structure than was Germany itself. If anything, it would be more correct to view Germany at this time as a microcosm of Europe as a whole,[1] encompassing both forward- and backward-looking elements prevalent throughout Europe, than as a clearly defined historical entity, nurturing a deep-rooted hostility toward the West. Like Europe itself, Germany was divided religiously between a Protestant North and a Catholic South. Politically, it was fragmented into several hundred sovereign states, ranging in importance from the major powers of Prussia and Austria to states sometimes no larger than private estates. Economically, Germany was mainly agrarian, and while it lagged behind the advanced areas of the West, owing to the shift in trade routes and the consequent decline of urban life since the sixteenth century, capitalism, especially in agriculture, and industry had made some headway in Prussia and elsewhere. Germany's cultural regeneration, beginning about 1750, and taking in the *Aufklärung, Sturm und Drang,* neohumanism, and the nascent movements of romanticism and idealism, would have been unthinkable without inspiration and influence from the West. Germany's cultural cosmopolitanism at this time accorded well with its actual position in Europe, signifying among other things the inspired but inadequate attempt by Germans to reconcile the old and the new without yielding decisively to either.

In effect, then, reactions to the French Revolution in Germany, and almost everywhere else for that matter, were reactions to modernity—in its Western, revolutionary, expansive phase. For wherever the Revolution made itself felt, in Spain and Russia as well as in Germany, it proved to be not just another instance of foreign intervention, which was nothing new in European political life. The Revolution also posed the problem of self-redefinition by the peoples it affected with regard to their own pasts and futures. The way in which the task of self-redefinition was handled in each case depended both upon the already existing condition of native institutions and traditions, and upon the ways in which the Revolution acted on them. Where they were vital, whether backward or not and whether "westernized" or not, resistance to the Revolution was comparatively strong and unequivocal, as in Spain, Russia, and the predominantly Germanic areas of the Habsburg Empire. Where they were weak, ineffectual, or already under sharp criticism, as in France first of all, as well as in Italy, Germany, and the predominantly non-Germanic parts of the Habsburg lands, the Revolution had a deeper and more problematical effect.

By 1815, after twenty-five years of upheaval, a more pronounced polarization between pro- and anti-Western forces existed everywhere. This polarization contributed in turn to a sharper cleavage, which proved to be irremediable thereafter, between the temporarily victorious and now more intransigent forces of reaction and the temporarily defeated and now more frustrated, revolution-prone forces of the future. These cleavages, which were only latent before 1789, came rapidly to the fore thereafter. Both before and after 1815 they existed *throughout* Europe, cutting across geographical, political, and cultural boundaries. This fact attested that neither westernism nor modernism during that time was a clearly defined or clearly definable notion and that the two were not, nor could yet be, neatly equated. These were the circumstances that set in motion the process of self-redefinition, a process that proved to be complicated everywhere, but nowhere more so than in Germany, where events had a deeper and more immediate impact than elsewhere.

There, even before the Revolution, the established but inept semifeudal order vied with newly revitalized but powerless cultural and intellectual currents, infused with modern ideas derived from the West. German approaches to the task of self-redefinition ranged, between 1789 and 1815, from reactionary romanticism (which identified the modern with the Western and repudiated both in favor of fanciful flights from actuality) to a modified classicism (which sought to transcend the cleavages between pro- and anti-westernism and between the modern and premodern). Between these two extremes were to be found less reactionary romantic poets, like Bettina von Arnim, Ludwig Tieck, and later Joseph von Eichendorff, Ludwig Uhland, Nikolaus Lenau, and Heinrich Heine, who were critical of certain facets of the modern without necessarily rejecting the West or joining the forces of reaction; and certain Prussian reformers, such as Karl vom Stein and Karl von Hardenberg, who sought to modernize Germany without surrendering totally to Western attitudes. To these may be added the philosophers of idealism, who considered *all* elements of the existing situation as necessary, but none as absolute, all being conceived as "moments" or phases interrelated dialectically in a total historical process which will only complete itself with the future appearance of a harmonious state of being. This outcome, they believed, will retain all essential elements of the past, but will not resemble it or any of its individual phases.

Hence, the vitality and distinctiveness of Germany's cultural and intellectual life during this period are to be explained by conditions at home as well as by events originating abroad. Just because Germany was a microcosm of Europe as a whole, it was bound to differ somewhat, especially in its cultural and intellectual disposition, from the comparatively well-defined and homogeneous Western nation-states as well as from the sprawling, polyglot empires and states of the East. For one thing, owing to the growth of Junker power, the political, social, and economic center of gravity of Germany had shifted since the sixteenth century from the southwest to the northeast, culminating in the most important European political development of the eighteenth century: the emergence of a powerful Prussia whose foundations lay outside the Holy Roman Empire and which was not subject, therefore, to the latter's traditions or authority. As this shift did not entail a corresponding shift in the cultural center of gravity, it meant one more fissure, that between the "westernized" centers of culture and the "easternized" centers of power, in a land already plagued by disunity.

As for the Holy Roman Empire, it remained the oldest surviving political structure in Europe, but had, since the Treaty of Westphalia, come to resemble an archaic "Gothic-Baroque edifice."[2] Never, since its inception almost a thousand years earlier, had its boundaries corresponded to those of Germany's national existence. It had either included large numbers of non-Germans or else had excluded large numbers of Germans. Hence another source of disunity by the eighteenth century: "Authority, so far as it existed, had no sympathy with national sentiment; national sentiment, so far as it existed, was opposed to authority."[3] Despite its long history of disservice to German national interests, however, the Holy Roman Empire remained, until its dissolution by Napoleon in 1806, "the last exiguous bond between the German peoples, the one remaining symbol of German unity."[4]

Even then, however, the reverie of German imperial greatness did not die, but found a new homeland in a Prussia that had become powerful by fusing the economic and military might of its agrarian capitalist Junker class with an efficient bureaucracy derived from the common European theory and practice of "enlightened" absolutism. There the memory of medieval German greatness illogically but effectively merged with modern nationalism, which first made its appearance as a progressive force in opposition to both the outmoded universalism and outmoded particularism on which that former imperial greatness had been based.

In the eighteenth century, however, Prussia was still an object of scorn, contempt, and fear. It was the land where Voltaire had hoped to find a true philosopher-king in the person of Frederick the Great, but found instead a neurotic *Machtpolitiker*, who grudgingly tolerated argument but insisted on obedience. It was the land Lessing called the most servile in Europe, and the one Herder considered the very embodiment of Leviathan. Prussia, even then, was the authoritarian state *par excellence*, the state whose genius lay in mobilizing the new to reinforce the old. It was the state in which culture and politics were so divorced from each other that the cultivated Francophile, Frederick the Great, felt prompted to remark in his own *Histoire de mon temps:* "I hope that posterity will do me justice and understand how to distinguish the king in me from the philosopher, the decent from the political man."[5] But Prussia was merely the most glaring example in eighteenth-century Germany of the disunity and mutual exclusion of culture and politics. In the long run this cleavage proved disadvantageous to both. But the fact that ideas did not yet pose a threat to German society made it possible for the cultural sphere to develop for a time relatively undisturbed, so long as it did not meddle in political or social affairs.

Political stagnation and disunity in turn discouraged social and economic progress. Whereas the two went hand in hand in the modern West, social and economic progress mutually resisted each other in Germany. The same forces which elsewhere strengthened the centralized state—the Reformation, the growth of capitalism and the corresponding decline of traditional feudal institutions, the creation of standing armies and efficient bureaucracies, and the spread of education—served in Germany only to reinforce a static and hierarchical political and social order.[6] The decline of urban life, increase in the power of the nobility, and "the feudalization of the great banking and merchant families into rentier groups living off a static economic system,"[7] all effectively combined to prevent the growth of a productive, self-respecting, cosmopolitan middle class. "Nothing would be more false than to see German burghers, between the sixteenth and eighteenth centuries, as modern, liberal, political citizens, as champions of social and political equality. Their basis, like the nobility's, was privilege and special rights."[8]

Instead, then, of the development of burgher pride and "class consciousness," instead of the growth of pressure groups and institutions, like the British Parliament or the French *parlements,* which could effectively influence national policy at times and bring middle class and aristocracy closer together, the divisions between the various classes and their interests hardened in Germany. There the middle class acquiesced in, and even identified its interests with, a semifeudal political and social system in which it would have to play a subservient role. Hence, the potentially progressive political class remained stunted in Germany, while the potentially conservative one came to include not only princes and nobles, but also urban patricians and guild masters.[9] And, until well into the nineteenth century, German literature continued to feature characters "whose life and outlook were still in all essentials those of the medieval guild craftsman."[10]

These conditions found expression, even before 1789, in various doctrines espousing the medieval ideal of an "organic," hierarchical state. Such doctrines appeared, for example, in the writings of Justus Möser (1720–1794), "the first knowledgeable and systematic traditionalist, the first great European reactionary."[11] Such reactionary views also served to discourage German progressive thinkers and writers from participation, and even from a desire to participate, in public affairs, and helped to mold them into the first "academic proletariat" in the modern sense. That is, they were, and felt themselves to be, estranged from both the aristocratic ruling classes, whose world view and way of life were incompatible with their ideals, and also from the burgher class in which most of them had originated. For while they tended to share the German burgher's "touching conscientiousness in holding things ignoble at a distance,"[12] and to some extent his stoic values—renunciation, thrift, duty, etc.—they consistently denounced his servility, stuffiness, and especially his "philistinism." In brief, they formed an isolated element that was politically, socially, and economically dispossessed. However, since neither they nor their ideas yet posed a threat to German society, they were a group that could be intellectually vigorous and ideologically independent.

These, then, were some of the principal factors that gave eighteenth-century German cultural and intellectual life its distinctive character. Germans lacked a national past to give them a sense of collective responsibility and purpose, and upon which writers might draw for inspiration and subject matter; a fact deplored by Goethe, for one, in his essay *Literary Sansculotism* (1795). It is no accident that such a large number of writings—Lessing's dramas, *Miss Sara Samson* (1755), *Emilia Galotti* (1772), *Nathan the Wise* (1779); Goethe's dramas, *Egmont* (1787), *Iphigenia in Tauris* (1787), and *Torquato Tasso* (1790); and most of Schiller's dramas—have non-German settings. As Walter Bruford has noted: "Cosmopolitanism was natural to men who had been allowed no political schooling and found little in 'fatherlands' like Württemberg or Weimar to satisfy their own political idealism."[13] Since Germany lacked a thriving middle class and capitalist economy, German thinkers were less prone than enlightened Westerners to adopt middle-class values. It is understandable, therefore, why that favorite eighteenth-century concept, Nature, rarely assumed in German thought the laissez-faire, mechanistic, eudaemonistic—modern bourgeois ideological—character it had acquired in the West. Nor is it surprising that German historicism, right from the start, in the writings of Möser and Johann Gottfried Herder (1744–1803), among others, defended the past, "the traditional freedoms of the Swiss, the estates of the Holy Roman Empire, and the traditions of Protestant spirituality, which are the bases of German historicism,"[14] against the present. This attitude was in contrast to the typical enlightened Western view of the past as a "collection of abuses and superstitions."[15]

German writers, unlike their Western counterparts who consciously represented broad sectors of society and could aspire to financial independence through writing, were still dependent upon patronage and clerical and university appointments. German writers wrote mainly for each other, for university professors and progressive bureaucrats, and for the marginal enlightened element of the middle classes and aristocracy. Since their ideas found little public support and had little public effect, many sought community and the opportunity for self-expression in the numerous secret societies that burgeoned in the eighteenth century. Almost every major progressive figure in the intellectual life of Germany during this period was a member of the Freemasons at one time or another. For the same reason they shared in the spirit of a rapidly spreading Pietism, which advocated spiritual inwardness, a mystical interpretation of Christianity and its application to practical life, and an elitist priesthood of believers which saw itself as a "Church invisible."

Small wonder, then, that German intellectuals usually concerned themselves less with what is than with what ought to be, and that it was to the realm of ideals that they made their most original and significant contributions. As progressive values were incompatible with Germany's retrograde social and political order, they tended to postulate sharp oppositions between the world of thought and that of social reality and to view the ideal world as more real than the physical one. Political freedom they conceived to be a consequence of spiritual perfection, and social progress the effect, rather than the cause, of cultural reform. Hence the frequent, and inevitably doomed, attempts to turn theaters, universities, and scholarly journals into instruments of national regeneration.

Progressive German writers and thinkers adhered to the characteristic Enlightenment values of intellectual self-reliance, self-fulfillment, the unity of natural and moral man, worldly well-being, and government by law, all of which they designated by the term *Humanität*. But since they proclaimed these values in a society unable to guarantee their realization by social or political action, those who favored progress were forced to consider other ways to bring it about. One of the most characteristic solutions they advanced was the concept of *Bildung,* a painstaking, precarious process of individual growth and self-definition whereby a person might bring his nascent humanity to fruition in a society that offered few aids and still fewer human models worthy of imitation.[16] It is noteworthy that the ideas of *Bildung* and the decline of the West (including Germany) gained currency more or less simultaneously and came to be considered as two sides of the same coin, as is evident in many of the writings of Herder, Humboldt, and Fichte.[17] In keeping with this line of thought, the artist was conceived to be the very epitome of *Bildung,* and rapidly became a favorite figure in German literature. For, depicted as an individualist who projected his personal human ideal as a general cultural one, the artist came to represent the healer and restorer of the world, the man who enacted and made his own the destiny of all mankind.[18] The concept of *Bildung* was Germany's finest expression of humanism, but as an attempt to view the world from the standpoint of the individual soul, it contained in embryo those false dichotomies between Culture and Civilization, between Community and Society, and between Spirit and Life which gained such prominence in Germany during the nineteenth and twentieth centuries.

This was the situation on the eve of the Revolution. As the Revolution ran its course from moderation to radicalism to retrenchment and, finally, to consolidation under Napoleon, it became increasingly clear that Germany could not follow France's example. The conditions for revolution simply did not exist east of the Rhine. Although the Revolution pointed up the justice of Germans' criticisms of their own country, it also demonstrated, as it degenerated into reaction and demagogy, its inability to create the conditions for freedom on German soil.[19] German progressives, those who had been in the forefront of the protest against their country's backwardness in the name of Enlightenment ideals, correctly concluded from these circumstances that the realization of their goals by means of revolution was out of the question.[20] German radicals were few, and those who, like Georg Forster (1754–1794) and Andreas Rebmann (1768–1824), held radical views, remained marginal figures. At best, progressive thinkers in Germany could realistically hope to keep their ideals alive only in a nonpolitical way, against both their feudal suppression at home and their bourgeois subversion from abroad.[21]

Moreover, as the Revolution made clear to antitraditionalist forces all over Europe that it was now at least possible to break with political absolutism, with its characteristic social institutions and cultural values, the Revolution also paved the way everywhere for the rise of nationalism and the emergence of a new tension in political life. This political development acted in turn as a stimulus to cultural innovation. Whereas, before 1789, cooperation with absolutism had been the only way in which progressives could hope to influence policy,[22] the dissociation of the identity of the state from the person of the dynast, signified by the execution of Louis XVI, now allowed for the merger of liberalism with nationalism. This development in turn generated a conservative reaction which now, for the first time, began to identify its interests with a strong monarchy. And, in the wake of this polarization between liberalism and conservatism, romanticism, as a protest against the cultural traditions of the *ancien régime,* arose to identify itself with the one or the other, depending upon which seemed better able to actualize its varying conceptions of the best interests of the "Volk." If, in the end, German romanticism tended predominantly to serve conservative interests, this was due in large part to the fact that conservatism succeeded during the Napoleonic period in appropriating the cause of German nationalism from the liberals. By the time of the Restoration, German romanticism was in the main conservative, while in France, where nationalism was still a liberal policy, romanticism also tended toward liberalism.

Even before the Revolution, however, some measure of national feeling existed throughout Europe.[23] Initially a liberal cause, nationalism emerged everywhere as a progressive force in opposition to the existing political and social order. In France and Germany, where this traditionalistic order was most detested by liberals, national feeling was correspondingly most antagonistic to it. In Germany especially, where political disunity made it necessary for nationalists to derive their doctrines from Germany's cultural unity, nationalism came to include everything opposed to the state, as is evident in the writings of Herder, the "father" of German nationalism.[24]

This belief in a common culture as the basis of nationhood was one important factor that, from the outset, differentiated German nationalism from nationalism elsewhere. But it easily led to the illusion that political and social change would follow more or less automatically from cultural reform. Many liberal nationalists, like Johann Gottlieb Fichte (1762–1814) and Wilhelm von Humboldt (1767–1835), applied themselves energetically to educational reform as a necessary precondition to nationhood. The result of such efforts, however, was not the one anticipated. Instead of contributing to the realization of a united liberal Germany, or even to a better preparation for participation in political affairs among the educated classes, the main result of such efforts was that, in the course of the nineteenth century, "the conflicts between education and life became increasingly bitter."[25] With Germany, as with most of the nations of the world, culture and education played a role in political unification, but not a role of leadership.

Another characteristic of German nationalism at this time was that German liberals, fearful of the still securely entrenched ruling classes, resisted the small but growing democratic demand for popular sovereignty. This fear cut them off from an important source of support and made them more amenable to an eventual alliance with conservatism. Also there existed no ready-made political structure, or even a feasible potential one, within which the goal of nationhood could be effected. For, until 1815, German liberals looked beyond the existing territorial states to a unified nation-state in which no one territory would dominate, in which the middle classes would supplant the aristocracy as the dominant social class, and in which all Germans (and only Germans) would be included—what later came to be known as the *grossdeutsch* or "greater German solution." To have carried out such a plan would have entailed a complete reordering of the European political map and an overhauling of Germany's social structure. Hence, this aspiration was wholly unrealistic, all the more so as German liberals had from the start rejected revolution as a legitimate means of historical change.

These factors help to explain why German liberalism failed to prevent the appropriation of the national cause by conservatives, who adapted it better to actual German conditions and, of course, to their own privileged interests. German conservatism, in reaction to liberalism's break with absolutism and Germany's defeat by Napoleon, now also began to favor a unified national state, but one in which Prussia and, hence, Junker interests, would predominate. Even reactionaries such as Ludwig von Marwitz (1777–1837), who, like the liberals, had grown discontented with bureaucratic absolutism, now began to subscribe to a form of nationalism that harkened back to Justus Möser's theory—a return to provincial patriotism, the situation that had prevailed before the rise of the centralized state and the preeminence of princely authority.

By 1815, then, three distinct interpretations of nationalism, derived from three mutually exclusive political theories, had emerged and were competing in Germany,[26] with the conservative version, the one most closely approximating the political *status quo*, ultimately winning out. Liberalism, because of its limited political base and lack of realism, and also because of the prestige that conservative Prussia had acquired by 1815 as the logical center for national regeneration, chose to support Prussia thereafter against the greater evil of Austria in their struggle for hegemony in Germany. This development marked the first great setback of German liberalism and one that foreshadowed its many later setbacks.

After twenty-five years of upheaval in Europe, German affairs were not much different from what they had been before. True, the Holy Roman Empire, and with it the mélange of ecclesiastical principalities, imperial cities, and knightly orders had been dissolved, but only to be replaced by a new and simpler system of political division—Austria, Prussia, and the German Confederation—which was confirmed by the Congress of Vienna. Nationalism remained confined mainly to Prussia and found effective expression only among the reformers, like Stein and Hardenberg, Scharnhorst and Gneisenau, who accomplished little more than to revitalize political absolutism by reaffirming and modernizing the traditional interdependence between monarchy and aristocracy. As Hans Rosenberg has summed it up:[27]

A streamlined system of political absolutism; a modified pattern of aristocratic privilege and social inequality; a redistribution of oligarchical authority among the revitalized segments of the traditional master class; a promotion of personal liberty and freedom of occupation and economic enterprise—these were the principal results of the bureaucratic saviours of Prussia.

Anti-Semitism also now emerged in force, since the French emancipation of Jews had come to be associated with foreign intervention, liberalism, and the defeat of Prussia, thus making them the obvious symbol of everything standing in the way of Germany's reconstruction along what were still semifeudal lines.[28] This was Germany on the eve of the Restoration, which the distinguished and representative historian of the period, Leopold von Ranke (1795–1886), referred to as "a reaction of the Nordic-Germanic world against the revolutionary Latin nations."[29]

The general effect of these twenty-five years on German cultural and intellectual life was to bring romanticism to the fore, to transform classicism from a theory of engagement into a personal refuge from, and barrier against, involvement in society and politics, and to transform idealism from the voluntaristic philosophy of Kant into the necessitarian system of Hegel. Ancient Greece, with its democratically inclined political form of the *polis,* its moral standard of the unity of the sensual and spiritual, and its aesthetic norm of "serene grandeur and noble simplicity," had been, for the early classicists Winckelmann, Herder, Goethe, and the early Schiller, a living symbol of humanity at its greatest, a symbol that could serve as the basis for the regeneration of modern society and culture. It now became, for the later Schiller and Hölderlin, an irretrievably lost ideal, something unrealizable in the present, a fading memory that might inspire, in poets and thinkers, "sentimental" striving but not "naive" attainment (Schiller's terms.)[30] *Bildung,* which originally had been conceived as a form of "joyful wisdom," accessible to any normal person, now begins to assume a nightmarish, Faustian quality, involving almost superhuman effort and self-sacrifice against a temporal process which, as in Goethe's *Faust,* ultimately destroys even the noblest of men. And faith in *Bildung* is abandoned altogether by romanticism, which replaces it with various forms of escape, solace, and yearnings for redemption from the world (e.g., Novalis' *Hymns to the Night,* 1800); and by the idealists, for whom the problem of self-definition becomes a problem of cosmic proportions, not an immediate individual possibility.

So, too, with the conception of Nature. Whereas, before the Revolution, German humanism envisaged Nature as man's ally in his quest for self-fulfillment, and man as the "pinnacle and reflection of Nature,"[31] it now becomes for Goethe a vision, for Schiller and Hölderlin a lost ideal, for Kant a limitation and source of evil, for Fichte a figment of the universal Ego, for Schelling a polarity to human existence, for Hegel a vestige of "dead consciousness," for Novalis an aesthetic fascination, for Eichendorff a source of consolation, for E. T. A. Hoffmann a specter, for Heine a sphinx and temptress. In all, the "great chain of being" theory gives way to a sense of man's estrangement from Nature. Art, history, philosophy, and science begin to function now as means to fill the void, either as alternatives to Nature or as ways of mastering it. Historicism, which had always held that there is a "fundamental difference between the phenomena of nature and those of history,"[32] now becomes, for the romantics, who contributed so greatly to the growth of historicism and its popularization among the educated, a principal means of self-recognition and orientation in a world where Nature no longer seemed to offer any assistance, and where art was now regarded as but the supreme expression of irony, a game of "transcendental buffoonery," as Friedrich Schlegel characterized modern romantic art. For Friedrich Carl von Savigny (1779–1861), for example, history becomes a substitute for Nature, a second nature; and in the writings of Ernst Moritz Arndt (1769–1860) and Ludwig "Turnvater" Jahn (1778–1852), culture is represented as a *natural* attribute, a conception with racist ramifications. *Naturphilosophie* and the biological sciences, physiology, cytology, etc., which flourished in Germany during these years, also represented efforts to restore the lost bonds between man and Nature through the discovery of new principles and patterns common to both.[33]

Germany? Where was it? It could not be found, so it had to be created. Nevertheless, Germany's various efforts at self-redefinition during these years were not just so many reflex reactions to general European events and conditions at home. On the contrary, at their highest cultural and intellectual level, in the best of classicism, romanticism, and idealism, these efforts exercised a formative influence on both the content and direction of modern culture as a whole. Much of subsequent nineteenth- and twentieth-century European culture found great inspiration in German romanticism. And, while German classicism never commanded wide support, even within Germany, and scarcely survived Goethe as a concerted philosophy of life, the stature and inspiration of the great figures of classicism and its humanist goals endured, as ideals if nothing else, in German higher learning and in the lives and writings of various scattered individuals. Finally, although the influence and importance of idealism fell off sharply after 1848, being supplanted thereafter by materialism and the anti-Hegelian philosophy of Schopenhauer, it penetrated as far afield as Britain and Russia, and, as is well known, served as the prime philosophical stimulus to Marxism. The turmoil of transition gave rise in Germany, as it has wherever modernity presents itself as a problem, to the need for self-redefinition. As products of this need, these three movements signified to Germans the best means by which to negotiate that transition. Seen in this light, their relevance and importance go far beyond their place of origin, marking Germany's most significant contribution to the very concept and content of the modern.

Notes to Chapter One

1. Viewing the whole of German history from this standpoint is one of the merits of the study by William J. Bossenbrook, *The German Mind* (Detroit: Wayne State University Press, 1961).
2. Carlo Antoni, *Der Kampf wider die Vernunft*, trans. from Italian by W. Goetz (Stuttgart: Koehler, 1951), p. 89.
3. A. J. P. Taylor, *The Course of German History*, 6th ed. (London: Methuen, 1966), p. 16.
4. Geoffrey Barraclough, *The Origins of Modern Germany*, 6th ed. (New York: Capricorn, 1963), p. 405.
5. Quoted in Karl Barth, *Protestant Thought: From Rousseau to Ritschl*, trans. by B. Cozens (New York: Harper, 1959), pp. 23–24.
6. Cf. Walter H. Bruford, *Germany in the Eighteenth Century*, 5th ed. (Cambridge, England: The University Press, 1965), pp. 3 ff.
7. Leonard Krieger, *The German Idea of Freedom* (Boston: Beacon, 1957), p. 36.
8. Friedrich Meinecke, *Das Zeitalter der deutschen Erhebung, 1795–1815*, 6th ed. (Göttingen: Vandenhoeck & Ruprecht, 1957), p. 25.
9. Klaus Epstein, *The Genesis of German Conservatism, 1770–1806* (Princeton, N.J.: Princeton University Press, 1966), pp. 47–48.
10. Bruford, *op. cit.*, p. 136.
11. Antoni, *op. cit.*, p. 101.
12. Gustav Freytag as quoted in Bruford, *op. cit.*, p. 229.
13. *Ibid.*, pp. 306–307.
14. Antoni, *op. cit.*, p. 6.
15. Georg G. Iggers, *The German Conception of History* (Middletown, Conn.: Wesleyan University Press, 1968), p. 33. See also Joachim Streisand, *Geschichtliches Denken von der deutschen Frühaufklärung bis zur Klassik*, 2nd rev. ed. (Berlin: Akademie-Verlag, 1967).
16. Cf. Walter H. Bruford, *Culture and Society in Classical Weimar, 1775–1806* (Cambridge, England: The University Press, 1962).

In an interesting appendix on the origin and meaning of the word *Bildung,* the author points out that it was not synonymous with "civilization" in the Western sense, nor did it mean *Kultur,* which is closer in meaning to "civilization." Rather, *Bildung* was more closely related to the French *la culture,* understood as personal cultivation. *Bildung* is "apparently the secularization of a term that goes back to the language of medieval mystics, and is connected with the idea of man being made in God's image (*Bild*), and striving to model himself on the image of Christ in his mind" (p. 438). The word *Kultur,* moreover, was slow to gain currency in Germany; the lexicographer Campe still regarded it, as late as 1807, as a word "imposed on the language" (p. 440). All of which serves to illustrate the German preference for a more spiritualistic and individualistic conception of culture than that conveyed by any other related word, whether native or borrowed.

17. Hans Weil, *Die Entstehung des deutschen Bildungsprinzips* (Bonn: Cohen, 1930), pp. 75–76.
18. Pierre Grappin, *La Théorie du Génie dans le Préclassicisme Allemand* (Paris: Presses Universitaires de France, 1952), pp. 273 ff.
19. Walter M. Simon, *Germany: A Brief History* (New York: Random House, 1966), pp. 78 ff.
20. Georg Lukács, *Brève Histoire de la Littérature Allemande,* trans. from German by L. Goldmann and M. Butor (Paris: Nagel, 1949), p. 59.
21. *Ibid.,* pp. 62 ff.
22. Fritz Valjavec, *Die Entstehung der politischen Strömungen in Deutschland, 1770–1815* (Munich: Oldenbourg, 1951), p. 153.
23. For historical background of German nationalism, see Valjavec, *ibid.,* pp. 328 ff. See also Reinhard Wittram, *Das Nationale als europäisches Problem* (Göttingen: Vandenhoeck & Ruprecht, 1954).
24. Antoni, *op. cit.,* Chapter 7.
25. Franz Schnabel, *Deutsche Geschichte im neunzehnten Jahrhundert,* 5th ed. (Freiburg im Breisgau: Herder, 1959), Vol. I, p. 433.
26. On these varieties of nationalism, see Walter M. Simon, "Variations in Nationalism during the Great Reform Period in Prussia," *American Historical Review, 59* (January, 1954), pp. 305–321.
27. Hans Rosenberg, *Bureaucracy, Aristocracy, and Autocracy: The Prussian Experience, 1660–1815* (Cambridge, Mass.: Harvard University Press, 1958), p. 203. On the Prussian reformers, see also Eugene N. Anderson, *Nationalism and the Cultural Crisis in Prussia, 1806–1815* (New York: Farrar & Rinehart, 1939); Guy Stanton Ford, *Stein and the Era of Reform in Prussia* (Princeton University Press, 1922); and Walter M. Simon, *The Failure of the Prussian Reform Movement* (Ithaca, N.Y.: Cornell University Press, 1955). On the relationship between reform and nationalism in Germany, see the two books by Jacques Droz, *L'Allemagne et la Révolution Française* (Paris: Presses Universitaires de France, 1949) and *Le Romantisme allemand et l'État* (Paris: Payot, 1966).
28. Reinhold Aris, *A History of Political Thought in Germany from 1789 to 1815* (London: Allen & Unwin, 1936), pp. 401–402.
29. *Ibid.,* p. 405.
30. For Schiller's use of these terms, see pp. 22–23. See also E. M. Butler, *The Tyranny of Greece over Germany* (Boston: Beacon, 1958), and Walther Rehm, *Griechentum und Goethezeit,* 3rd ed. (Munich: Lehnen, 1952).
31. Mario Pensa, *Das deutsche Denken,* trans. from Italian by W. Meckauer (Erlenbach-Zurich: Rentsch, 1948), p. 88. See also Wladyslaw Folkierski, *Entre le Classicisme et le Romantisme* (Paris: Champion, 1925), Part 3. See also Grappin, *op. cit.*
32. Iggers, *op. cit.,* p. 4.
33. Alexander Gode-von Aesch, *Natural Science in German Romanticism* (New York: Columbia University Press, 1941). Stephen F. Mason, *A History of the Sciences,* rev. ed. (New York: Collier, 1962), Chapters 29–32.

These three movements overlapped and intermingled both in time and in conceptual content. Their differences were more a matter of emphases than clear-cut distinctions. Accordingly, some of the greatest figures of the period during which these movements reached their culminations cannot be neatly fitted into any of them. Friedrich Hölderlin (1770–1843) and the early Friedrich Schlegel (1772–1829) thought of themselves more as continuators of classicism than as its opponents. Scarcely anyone escaped the influence of Kantian idealism. Goethe, despite his famous repudiation of romanticism as "sickness," was fully capable of creating romantic moods and characters, such as Mignon and the Harper in *Wilhelm Meister's Apprenticeship.* And what is Faust's pact with Mephistopheles if not the "classical" expression of romanticism? Almost all of Goethe's writings contain some elements of romanticism; almost none, however, can be called romantic in the final analysis. Hegel in turn was capable of speaking in the voices of both classicism and romanticism, though never fully on their own terms; and speaking with yet a third voice, that of the World-Spirit which, he thought, both engendered and resolved dialectically such apparently contradictory developments as these two movements within the context of world history as a whole.

One reason for the interrelation of these three movements is that they all originated and took shape within a comparatively short time-span, from approximately 1780 to 1800. None had an opportunity to establish itself as orthodoxy and, consequently, none as heresy; hence, the absence of sharp oppositions among them, such as existed between classicism and romanticism in France. By the same token, all matured during the same historical phases in Germany—stagnation, upheaval, and reconstruction—and so addressed themselves to a more or less common set of problems and circumstances.

CLASSICISM, ROMANTICISM, AND IDEALISM AS ORIENTATIONS

The movements differed in that classicism was more deeply rooted in the stagnant, but comparatively stable, conditions of prerevolutionary Germany; romanticism in the highly volatile conditions of the revolutionary era itself; and idealism in the period of reconstruction.

This does not mean that the finest products of these movements were conceived during their respective periods of origination. Goethe's and Schiller's greatest works were written during and after the Revolution; Kant and Fichte were writing idealist philosophy before and during the Revolution; and romanticism lingered on long after the Revolution. It does mean, however, that each received its most forceful stimuli and formulated its characteristic orientation during these various phases. Thus, even though Goethe's two masterpieces, *Wilhelm Meister* and *Faust*, were completed, the one during and the other long after the Revolution, there is scarcely any reference to it in them; and Schiller makes only passing mention of events in his *Aesthetic Letters*, which were written at the very height of the Revolution, between 1793 and 1795. Both men were, of course, perfectly aware of what was happening. Much later Goethe would claim, in his *Campaign in France* (1822), that he had witnessed at the cannonade of Valmy (1792) the start of a new epoch in world history.

However, since both of these leading representatives of classicism had already rejected revolution as a valid means of change, they found themselves seeking alternatives to it in its very midst. The Revolution seemed to them to pose as many problems as it solved, problems similar to those which had existed before and would continue to exist after 1789, such as the absence of harmony and purpose in contemporary European society, the continuation of political tyranny and social injustice, and the ill effects of collectivization and specialization on human life. Accordingly, they sought a frame of reference for dealing with such problems broader than that provided by the Revolution itself. Likewise, even though Adalbert von Chamisso's marvelous romantic tale *Peter Schlemihl* appeared as late as 1814 and also makes no reference to the Revolution, it is almost wholly preoccupied with the drastic dislocation of the individual and the breakdown of a solid sense of selfhood, which were the direct effects of the Revolution. Finally, even though Hegel's *Phenomenology of Mind* was completed as early as 1806, it rings with the author's belief in the originality and newness of the philosophy contained therein, its value for the future, for an age which had to contend with a new Europe and a new Germany, a Germany smashed by Napoleon's armies that very year. Why, then, these different orientations and what did they signify?

Schiller and His Contemporaries on Art and Society

The palaces of the kings are now closed. The
tribunals have withdrawn from the gates of the
cities to the interiors of houses; the letter has
crowded out the living word; the people itself, that
palpable vibrant mass, when it does not act as a
raw force, has become the state, and hence an
abstract idea; and the gods have returned within the
bosom of man. The poet must reopen the palaces,
bring the tribunals out in the open air, resurrect the
gods; he must restore everything immediate which
has been abolished by the artificial arrangements of
contemporary life.

Schiller

Although the high point of German classicism came during the decade of Goethe and Schiller's close friendship and fruitful collaboration, 1794 to 1805, it was more deeply rooted in the cultural traditions of prerevolutionary Europe than the other two movements. Long before the Revolution, both writers had become adherents to the values of the Enlightenment and had shared in the *Sturm und Drang* protest against Germany's backward condition. They had been nurtured on the writings of Spinoza and Leibniz, Winckelmann and Lessing, Hamann and Herder, Diderot, and above all Rousseau. Thus they were already firmly committed to the value of reason, thought of not only as the power of "analyzing and dissecting," but also as the power capable of "actually bringing about that order of things which it conceives as necessary, so that by this act of fulfillment it may demonstrate its own reality and truth."[1] They were committed to the standard of artistic excellence best represented by the ancient Greeks (but not only by them); to Nature conceived as a universal moral and spiritual norm; to a belief in the immanence of universal values in human nature and in history; and to the ideal of harmony within and between all men. This was the substance of their cosmopolitanism.

With the coming of the French Revolution, the chief question in their minds was no longer whether these values they had derived from the Enlightenment were still valid, but whether and how they might be implemented within this new historical setting. As the Revolution progressed from a civil war, aimed at the internal reorganization of France, to an international struggle, involving broad social and national issues, their attention turned from the mere assertion of these ideas to the task of determining what modifications they would have to undergo to survive and what shape society would have to assume to accommodate them. Although both men regarded the middle classes and the German nation as victims of the *ancien régime,* neither, for reasons stated earlier, saw fit to identify his values with their interests and existence. On the contrary, the German *Aufklärung* differed from the Western Enlightenment precisely in that its critique of society already implied a criticism of the middle classes as well as of the aristocracy, and that it confined itself to a mainly cultural conception of nationhood. Consequently, insofar as the French Revolution proved in the end to be as much a struggle for specifically bourgeois and national interests as for the realization of *liberté, égalité,* and *fraternité,* neither Goethe nor Schiller felt bound to defend these interests or to yield their cosmopolitan values in the face of them. At the same time, these interests became factors to be reckoned with.

In the emerging German classicism of the midnineties, therefore, we find that what was earlier thought to be clearly defined has now become problematical. The art of Goethe and Schiller now no longer merely depicts ready-made humanist heroes in conflict with an inhuman society, such as we find in Goethe's *Werther* (1774) and *Tasso* (1790), or in Schiller's *Intrigue and Love* (1783) and in his histories of the late eighties and early nineties. The arts had now to educate and activate the disaffected elements of society, to complete and perfect history, i.e., to assume a quasi-political function. As historian, Schiller was primarily concerned with learning "what we are, what we have become." Once he lost confidence in the ability of the French Revolution to effect its own humanistic program, he came to see the chief task of the age to make clear "what we are not, but are to become and should become."[2] It was then, in 1793, that he abandoned his career in history to return to art.

For Schiller and Goethe both, the arts were now to serve as the "correctors of history."[3] To do so, the arts had to be immersed in history in such a way as to reveal its positive potentialities. The dramas Schiller wrote during this period, which are among his greatest, the *Wallenstein* trilogy (1797), *Mary Stuart* (1800), and the *Maid of Orleans* (1802), are those in which the ideal emerges from and works itself out within the real. His one important play of this time based on pure myth, *Wilhelm Tell* (1804), is, for all its charm and popularity, the weakest artistically, suffering from oversimplification. Goethe, too, for whom history as a branch of knowledge had never ranked very high, would complete *Wilhelm Meister's Apprenticeship* (1796), the first and most representative example of the *Bildungsroman; Hermann and Dorothea* (1797), the great German poem of the French Revolution; and return to work on part one of *Faust* (1808). For both, art was now to substitute for and also "correct" the national middle-class revolution that would not and could not occur in Germany.

Friedrich Schiller (1759–1805) developed these thoughts into a program in his letters *On the Aesthetic Education of Man* (1793–1795). He states at the outset that aesthetic education is a means, not an end, a means to bring about "the most perfect of all works of art, the building up of true political freedom." The chief obstacle in the way of achieving this goal is the emerging modern form of necessity: "Utility . . . the great idol of the age, to which all powers must do service and all talents swear allegiance."[4] To overcome this obstacle, and to formulate the conception of a state of being good and desirable in and of itself, was Schiller's objective in these letters.

For the content of this program of aesthetic education, he drew mainly from two sources: from Kant, who held that the basic problem of civilization is a deep-rooted conflict between man's (evil) natural impulses and his (good) moral ones, a conflict that will be resolved only when "art will be strong and perfect enough to become a second nature."[5] Schiller drew also from Goethe, who believed, in contrast to Kant, that human nature is basically unified, and that the passions, which are fundamentally good, need only be ennobled and humanized by art. To synthesize these two positions—to show how human nature can be transformed and educated to reason, but without suppressing or doing violence to its ideal unity—this was Schiller's objective.

Like Kant, he envisaged history as the progress of mankind from nature which, although a realm of necessity, had at least preserved man's unity of being at a primitive level, to society, where this original unity has been destroyed, to a future state, in which it will be restored at a higher level. In this final phase, the sensuous and moral aspects of human nature both will be able to assert their claims and yet coexist in harmony. Schiller differed from Kant, however, in attributing the disunity of historical man not to an original conflict between natural impulse and morality, but, like Rousseau and Goethe, to the defects of culture itself. The first few letters, which describe the abject condition of man in contemporary society, still ring with the spirit of Rousseau:[6]

It was culture itself that inflicted the wound upon modern humanity. As soon as enlarged experience and more precise speculation made necessary a sharper division of the sciences, on the one hand, and on the other hand, the more intricate machinery of States made necessary a more rigorous dissociation of ranks and occupations, the essential bond of human nature was torn apart, and a ruinous conflict set its harmonious powers at variance.

Throughout these letters, Schiller's line of thought seems to be that play is productive of beauty, beauty, of harmony, harmony, of freedom, and freedom, in turn, conducive to play. Art as the educator of man to freedom and human wholeness, best exemplified

THE ROMAN HOUSE IN THE WEIMAR PARK, engraving by G. M. Krauss
An architectural expression of the classicist ideal of calm grandeur and noble
simplicity.

by the ancient Greeks, seemed feasible to Schiller because it is "an
instrument which the State does not afford us" and enjoys "an
absolute immunity from human lawlessness."[7] Art is possible,
therefore, where politics is not. It can serve as a substitute for
politics in emancipating man from the fetters of history and re-
covering his lost totality, which the state after all has been mainly
responsible for destroying. Although the education of man to freedom through art was not a new idea in aesthetic theory, hitherto
it had remained in the background. Through Schiller it now became,
as an alternative to political and social revolution, central to a whole
tradition of German thought in search of some other guarantee of
reality to the political creation of reason.

Having dealt with the purpose of art in his *Aesthetic Education*,
Schiller turned to the question of what forms of art might best
serve it. In his next essay on aesthetics, *Naive and Sentimental Poetry*
(1795), a penetrating analysis of a variety of art forms and their
peculiar characteristics, he developed his famous distinction between what he believed to be the two *fundamental* poetic types, or
"modes of feeling" (*Empfindungsweise*), as he terms them. One, the
naive poet, is in harmony with nature; the other, the sentimental
poet, can only project it as an ideal. The two, who actually embody
antithetical species of poetry corresponding to two antithetical types
of human kind, represent for Schiller a typology of basic human

temperaments: an antithesis "without doubt as old as the beginnings of civilization and scarcely to be overcome before its end. . . ."[8] The naive poet, predominant in Greek antiquity but not confined exclusively to it, succeeds in embodying in his art the creativity, spontaneity, and self-consistency characteristic of the objects of nature in relation to us: "They are what we were; they are what *we should once again* become."[9] The sentimental poet, predominant in modern civilization and denatured by it, can only represent the naive attainment as an ideal, either in satire, elegy, or in the idyll, all of which represent in different ways modern man's estrangement from nature. Naive poetry is "the art of finitude"; sentimental poetry, "the art of the infinite."[10]

It is clear from the way in which Schiller develops his distinction that preference thus far in history goes to the naive poet, who alone can claim genius. "Every true genius must be naive, or it is not genius. Only its naivety makes for its genius . . . ."[11] In proclaiming the superiority of naive over sentimental poetry, however, he did not intend to "depreciate the moderns," since the path of modern poetry is "that along which man in general, the individual as well as the race, must pass," and also because "the goal to which man in civilization *strives* is infinitely preferable to that which he *attains* in nature."[12] Schiller conceived the two as antithetical modes of feeling inherent in civilization itself, rather than as historical styles which die with the expiration of the civilizations wherein they flourished. Believing this, he was able to avoid the conclusion that naive poetry, the only poetry of genius caliber, is impossible in the modern world, and also to envisage both types of poetry as components of a future synthesis. For neither "quite exhausts the ideal of beautiful humanity that can only arise out of the intimate union of both."[13]

However, if the two are mutually exclusive (at least in principle), how could naive poets exist in the modern world and sentimental poets in the ancient? If not, why did the one predominate in antiquity and the other only later? It seems that Schiller was unable to decide whether his "modes of feeling" were philosophical or historical categories. If the former, why did naive poetry ever give way to sentimental poetry in the first place? If the latter, how was it able to survive beyond the limits of classical civilization and be expected to figure in a future synthesis with its more predominant opposite?

This was the theoretical dilemma Schiller's argument posed. His dilemma was not, however, due to incompetence on his part as either philosopher or historian. On the contrary, this essay is rich in insights into the relationships between art and society, and between literary form and content; and his analyses of specific authors and writings are generally consistent with his categories and illuminated by them. But he did tend to confuse philosophical with historical categories, and this for two reasons. On the one hand, in the absence of any concrete historical guarantee for the realization of his future aesthetic state, he could only seek a guarantee for it in the transhistorical realm, in the supposed timelessness of his modes of feeling.[14] On the other hand, only history seemed able to explain why naive poets "are no longer at home in this artificial age. They are indeed scarcely even possible, at least in no other wise possible except that they *run wild* in their own age, and are preserved by some favorable destiny from its crippling influence."[15]

This dilemma prevented Schiller from explaining the very thing his theory was supposed to explain; namely, how sentimental poetry, the antithesis of the naive, was to serve dialectically as the vehicle for its ultimate resurrection. And this dilemma signified the defect in his plan to transform German society by way of aesthetic education. For Schiller to have confined himself to deriving his categories empirically, by abstracting the essentials from ancient and modern literature, would, by his own theory, have spelled the doom of the naive. To avoid this, he attempted a transmutation of his time-bound categories into timeless modes of feeling, then reintroduced them into time *sub specie aeternitatis*. It seems—and this is the failing implicit in Schiller's theory, in German classicism as a whole—that he either had to relinquish his genuine, powerfully expressed humanist ideals, or else perform this philosophical operation on history. He chose the latter course.

Of all the classicists, only the complicated Friedrich Hölderlin, who was inspired by Schiller above all, and who was his only peer or superior in poetic articulation of the Greek experience, grasped the defect in Schiller's position. Hölderlin realized that the appropriation by Germany or by modern mankind in general of the Greek aesthetic ideal would necessarily require also the appropriation of the Greek social experience, as a prior condition for its attainment. Hölderlin's "Graecomania" (Schiller's term) was based on the sound insight that the ideal cannot be disengaged from its historical setting without doing violence in the process to the ideal itself. This was especially true, he believed, in the case of the one civilization whose greatness and power to inspire modern mankind lay precisely in its alleged unity. Lamenting the loss of Greek greatness, he wrote:[16]

Dead and gone is she who nursed and stilled me,
Lovely, youthful world, she's dead and gone,
And the joy with which the heavens filled me;
Dead this breast, and barren like a stone.

Though the spring still sings to charm my sorrow
As before a sweet consoling song,
Yet departed is my life's fair morrow
And the springtime of my heart is gone.

Hölderlin's uncompromising adoration of the Greeks, far from being illiberal or antimodern—and this is one reason Schiller and the other Weimar classicists shunned him—signified an implicit criticism of any attempt, however well-meaning, to adapt Greek ideals to modern conditions which could no longer possibly sustain them. On the contrary, his work represents the juncture at which German classicism had to make the choice between service to a hopeless political attempt to transform Germany in accordance with the Greek experience or surrender to the anti-classical spirit of romanticism. Hölderlin, whose life ended in insanity, advocated the first course. His protagonist, Hyperion, exclaims:[17]

I will take a shovel and throw the dung into a pit. A people among whom spirit and greatness no longer engenders any spirit and any greatness has nothing in common with other peoples who are still men, has no more rights; and it is an empty farce, sheer superstition, to go on honoring such will-less corpses as if a Grecian heart beat in them. Away with them! The withered, decaying tree shall not stand where it stands, it steals light and air from the young life that is ripening for a new world!

Schiller, who sought to protect his Greek-inspired conception of beauty by defining it as "a completely closed creation" in which "there is no force to contend with force, no unprotected part where temporality might break in,"[18] found himself drifting toward the second course, surrender to romanticism. Just about a hundred years later, Tolstoy, also in search of a sound philosophical theory of art applicable to the modern world, clearly perceived the shortcoming in Schiller's position, which Hölderlin had sought to avoid: "By referring the judgments of the ancients on beauty to our conception of it . . . , we give the words of the ancients a meaning which is not theirs."[19]

This dilemma of German classicism carried over into the early romantic reinterpretation of Schiller's categories, which was best formulated by Friedrich Schlegel. He, like Schiller, began as a classicist and student of Kant's philosophy, sharing with both a belief in the existence of universally valid aesthetic precepts.[20] In 1796, however, prompted by his reading of Schiller's *Naive and Sentimental Poetry,* Schlegel too turned to the question of the relationship between ancient and modern literature. His own previous research had already convinced him that classical civilization was too far removed from the modern for its aesthetic standards, however praiseworthy, to serve as models for contemporary art. He continued to hold to Schiller's distinction between naive and sentimental poets, which he renamed classical and romantic. But the change in name also signified a change in meaning. For Schlegel, they no longer represented universal human types, but rather different cultural styles, corresponding to two different ages and to two different sets of historical conditions. Accordingly, he concluded that the modern (romantic) neither can nor should seek to model itself on the ancient (classical). In thus historicizing Schiller's universal modes of feeling, Schlegel abandoned altogether their dialectical relationship and their possible synthesis in the future.

But the differences between the two run deeper. Where Schiller idealizes the historical, Schlegel historicizes the ideal. Where Schiller separates ideal and reality too sharply, Schlegel identifies them too closely. In the one, the absolute dissolves the particular; in the other, the particular absorbs the absolute. Schlegel modifies Schiller's notion of the "infinite striving" of the sentimental poet in such a way as to identify it with little more than an exhaustive representation of actuality in all its diversity and transiency. In this respect his conception of the "romantic" is not merely the equivalent of Schiller's "sentimental"; it assimilates the principal characteristics of the "naive" as well, claiming to be in effect an "art of finitude" as well as an "art of the infinite." For Schlegel's famous definition of romantic poetry as a "progressive universal poetry"[21] means that it is progressive in the sense of being as yet incomplete, still striving toward the ideal (understood as the restoration of man's unity with nature); and universal in that it is cumulative, all-embracing, *inclusive* of the naive as well as of the sentimental striving after it. Romantic art should aim, therefore, to be a "total art" (*Gesamtkunst*), mixing every sort of genre, naive and sentimental alike, and every sort of subject matter (*Bildungs-stoff*), the real and imaginary, past and present, the timeless and time-bound, "even the degenerate types of poetry—the eccentric and the monstrous."[22] This actually became the aim of Novalis' incoherent novel *Heinrich von Ofterdingen* (1800), and Schlegel's own nondescript novel *Lucinde* (1800).

Thus, while Schlegel's theory derives from Schiller's, it also turns out to be a repudiation of it. Where Schiller calls for an art of the natural, Schlegel and the early German romantics consider *art to be natural*. Where Schiller holds that great art is possible only in defiance of the conditions of modern life, Schlegel professes that only these conditions, and the artist's personal responses to them, make it possible. Where Schiller asserts that "because the ideal is an infinitude to which he never attains, the civilized man can never become perfect in *his* own wise, while the natural man can in his,"[23] Schlegel produced what he called "a very spendid justification of the modern."[24]

In this antithesis, "one of the most radical that modern thought and taste have to show,"[25] we find the chief historical significance of the romantic reaction to classicism in Germany. For Schlegel's theory, in challenging both Schiller's sharp contrast between the real and ideal and his overriding emphasis on universals, in recognizing that *all* great art since antiquity has, in fact, managed to unite both the naive and sentimental in a single creative process, marks a definite advance over Schiller's theory. However, in lapsing into relativism, in substituting a personal for a universal perspective on reality, romanticism proved no better able than classicism to surmount the opposition between the real and ideal basic to both theories. By failing to recognize that this conflict could only be resolved by the transformation of political and social reality itself, the classical aesthetics of criticism simply gave way to the romantic aesthetics of accommodation. Once romanticism became discontent with the world as it was, which happened, understandably, more quickly and thoroughly in Germany than elsewhere, it found itself with no alternative other than flight from the world by way of the artistic imagination. For in committing itself so completely to the present, romanticism found that it had deprived itself of any other means of resisting or transcending reality once disaffection set in. And nowhere does this tragic dilemma of German thought at that time find better expression than in the prescient conclusion to Schiller's essay *Naive and Sentimental Poetry:*[26]

If . . . true idealism is insecure and often dangerous in its effects, false idealism is appalling in its effects. The true idealist abandons nature and experience only because he does not find in it the immutable and unconditional necessity for which his reason prompts him to strive; the fantast abandons nature out of pure caprice, in order to indulge with all the less restraint the wantonness of his desires and the whims of his imagination. . . . For the very reason that his phantasmagoria is not a deviation from nature but from freedom, and this develops out of a capacity in itself estimable and infinitely perfectible, it leads likewise to an infinite fall into a bottomless abyss and can only terminate in complete destruction.

Goethe and the Problem of *Bildung*

Both Schiller and Schlegel had high praise for the novel by Johann Wolfgang von Goethe (1749–1832), *Wilhelm Meister's Apprenticeship* (1796); Schiller because it seemed to exemplify his theory of aesthetic education, and Schlegel because it seemed to achieve that full description of the actual and fusion of the classical and romantic called for by *Universalpoesie.* Both were partly right. Goethe shared with both of them the view that human wholeness—the resolution of the conflict between moral and natural man, between thought and action, between sentimental striving and naive attainment—should be, and in the best cases is, the origin and goal of all human development. Unlike Schiller, however, Goethe believed that this aspiration is not merely an abstract Idea in the Kantian sense, but an inherent and ever-present potentiality of human nature itself. It is an *Urerlebnis,* a *primal* experience, to be sure; rare, remote, and pure, similar to a Platonic recollection. But it is a primal *experience* as well, one potentially within the reach of anyone at any time under any circumstances. Whereas, for Schiller, man's unity of being can only be a future acquisition, for Goethe it is his full and spontaneous self-manifestation in the present. Schiller grounded his view in a philosophy of dialectical dualism; Goethe conceived man as a microcosm of nature conceived as an all-embracing creative process. For Schiller, following Kant, the universal both is and is known to be universal and maintains its integrity as a universal only because it is distinct from and logically prior to the particular. For Goethe, the universal is such because it derives from nature, which is universal, and is, therefore, inherent in all individual beings in some form and to some extent. The universal is *in* the particular or it is nowhere.

The differences between the two thinkers would seem to suggest that Goethe's novel leans more in the direction of Schlegel's thinking, except that both classicists were primarily concerned with bringing about a universally valid human condition, a similarly conceived humanism. The author of *Wilhelm Meister,* for all that he delighted in the actual, the individual, the nuance, in the ironic exposé of the discrepancy between intention and deed, thought and feeling, the ideal and the real, rarely delighted in them for their own sake. For all of his mixing of literary genres, including "even the degenerate types of poetry," and mixing of character types, ranging from the stodgy burgher Werner to the hauntingly exotic Mignon and the Harper—for all that, his main purpose was not, like Schlegel's in *Lucinde,* to "fill and cram" his work with "every sort of solid *Bildungsstoff* and animate the whole with the play of humor."[27]

Finally, for all that Goethe strove to make *Wilhelm Meister* a "total" work of art, to effect a fusion of the naive and sentimental, it was the admiring Schiller who, after comparing it to a "beautiful planetary system," observed that Mignon and the Harper "run wholly out of this system, and, after having merely served to produce a poetical movement in it, separate themselves from it as foreign individuals."[28] Novalis (*né* Friedrich von Hardenberg, 1772–1801), the novel's most hostile but most acute critic, effectively confirmed Schiller's judgment by characterizing the novel as "modern. The romantic in it is destroyed—also the natural poetry and the wondrous. It deals merely with common *human* matters—nature and mysticism are completely neglected."[29] Schlegel was mistaken in thinking Mignon—the embodiment of the romantic, the wondrous, the mystical, and presumably the personification of the fusion of the naive and sentimental (symbolized perhaps by her hermaphroditic traits)—to be "the mainspring" of the work.[30] In fact, she is an abortive personification of that fusion who, in her insatiable longing for the unattainable, can neither function in the world nor find appreciation in it. And Goethe's treatment of this extraordinary creature turns out to be a devastating attack on romanticism itself, on its solipsism, on the attempt, undertaken by Novalis in his *Heinrich von Ofterdingen* (which was deliberately written to refute Goethe's novel), to make "the world become a dream, the dream become the world."[31]

What makes this attack so devastating is that Goethe turns romanticism against itself, making Mignon and the Harper emerge as "unnatural" creatures, victims of their own "theoretically monstrous . . . abortions of the understanding" (Schiller),[32] and finally the architects of their own destruction—Goethe outdoing even the romantic writers when he put his mind to it. Not the least merciless part of the attack is that Wilhelm, Goethe's own advocate, is unwittingly the immediate cause of Mignon's death, which is quickly forgotten by all. This cruel treatment of her prompted Schiller to remark: "Mignon's death, although we are prepared for it, affects one powerfully and deeply, so deeply, in fact, that many will think you quit the subject too abruptly. . . . It strikes one as odd that, directly upon the scene of her affecting death, the doctor should make an experiment upon her corpse, and that this living being should so soon be able to forget the person, merely in order to regard her as an instrument of scientific inquiry."[33] This gruesome end to Mignon, which actually only endorses Schiller's own thoughts on the fate of "fantasts,"[34] may also be read, however, as a brilliant caricature of romantic irony. For what could be more ironical than to make this poetic creature an "instrument of scientific inquiry" at the hands of her antipodes?—a true *coincidentia oppositorum*. And what more ironical than that the experiment should be her embalming, as if to accentuate her un-lifelike qualities by retaining in her "a look of life"?[35]

But Mignon does not "run wholly out" of the system of *Wilhelm Meister*. Nor, on the other hand, is she its "mainspring." And, while Novalis clearly perceived what the novel was attacking, he chose to ignore what it defended. It seems that Mignon only appeared in the novel at all as a manifestation of that "second" soul that Goethe claimed dwelled within his breast, as if to illustrate that classicism and romanticism are each other's alter-ego, and that where the one thrives, the other fails. So long as historical progress seemed a reality to Goethe, so long as the French Revolution seemed to him "the first dawn of the sun . . . when were heard the rights of man common to all men, heard the freedom inspiring to all, and equality worthy of praise,"[36] his "second" soul could be effectively contained. Poor Mignon, too fragile and inept to cope with herself or the world and no match for Wilhelm or the other educators in this novel, remains on the periphery. Once, however, the pendulum swung to reaction and counterrevolution set in, with German romanticism leading the way, Mignon, as if returning to avenge herself, metamorphoses as it were into the worldly, domineering, masculine Mephistopheles, who is every bit Faust's equal. And her tender ballad [37]

Know'st thou the land where citron-apples bloom,
And oranges like gold in leafy gloom,
A gentle wind from deep-blue heaven blows,
The myrtle thick, and high the laurel grows?
    'Tis there! 'Tis there
O my true loved one, thou with me must go!

evolves into Mephistopheles' sneering, cynical, magical proposition:[38]

I'll bind myself to be your servant here
And at your beck and call wait tirelessly,
If when there in the yonder we appear
You will perform the same for me.

Not Mignon, then, but the opposite of what she represents is at the center of *Wilhelm Meister:* the quest for the realization of humanist ideals within a constricting and degraded social order. For the chief question Goethe raises here, the one around which *all* the characters in the novel revolve, is what a person must be, what qualities and insights he must possess, to enable him to relate to a dehumanizing society without either being destroyed by it or compromising with it. The solution, the whole point of Wilhelm's "apprenticeship," lay, for Goethe, in the cooperation between art and action; because only the artist, with his microcosmic "fellow-feeling of the mournful and joyful in the fate of all human beings,"[39] is able to inspire truly human deeds, and only the man of action is able to translate the artist's vision into reality. Art and action are, for Goethe, but two aspects of the same thing, what he might have called a "primal" human type; for art is impotent unless it leads to action, and action blind unless inspired by art. "Thus by its power does the magnet join/Things iron with things iron together/As equal striving joins heroes and poets."[40] This

GOETHE IN THE CAMPAGNA, portrait by Johann F. A. Tischbein
This famous portrait captures the greatest figure of Weimar classicism in a characteristic pose and setting.

combination of hero and poet is what Goethe understood by genius, which, for him, was nothing more than the normal man fully developed. It was a theme which preoccupied him throughout his life, and a direct line links his Werther and Tasso, Goetz von Berlichingen and Egmont with Wilhelm Meister and Faust.

In all cases Goethe's objective was to build a bridge between the personal and public spheres of life. In all cases it was the abject condition of German society which frustrated that endeavor, whether in the form of a boorish, pompous nobility, for whom human conduct is judged only according to externalities, or that of a servile, philistine burgher class, whose subjugation to utility and overspecialization precludes the full and harmonious development of the individual. To steer between the two toward that goal, to master (*meistern*) reality, dependent only upon his own resources and experiences, is Wilhelm's one and only personal objective and the aim of his apprenticeship. This quest, the success or failure to fulfill it, is the sole criterion by which the vast array of characters and human types in this novel are judged. In those who succeed, like Jarno and the abbé, Lothario and Nathalie, and Wilhelm himself, we find the expression of Goethe's characteristic faith in man's ability to create a life of compassion, understanding, and purposeful activity, arrived at in a spirit and environment of spontaneity and sociability. In those who fail, like Werner and Laertes, Aurelia and Mignon, we find his condemnation not only of the established social order, but also of any ineffectual revolt against it, which succeeds only in leaving it intact.

Wilhelm Meister's Apprenticeship was Goethe's translation into literature, into the first and finest specimen of the educational novel (*Bildungsroman*), of Schiller's theory of aesthetic education. As with Schiller, Goethe's conception of the aesthetic was intended to be not an end in itself, but rather the one seemingly possible means to achieve in Germany the goals proclaimed by the French Revolution. At the same time, as with Schiller, his vision for humanity in this novel was bound to end in a utopian impasse. For the very conditions that gave rise to this German brand of humanism were the same ones that precluded its realization. Thus, while Goethe allows Wilhelm and some others to find self-fulfillment in the end, he realistically allows this to happen only within the confines of a humanist utopia made up of an unrepresentative elite of enlightened aristocrats and bourgeois who, in the interest of self-preservation and the propagation of their ideals, set themselves apart from society at large. The fragile balance of forces attempted in this writing, its tightrope walk between accommodation and action, between adaptation and improvisation, between art as serving life and life art, soon broke down and polarized into the "educational novel" of escape (Novalis' *Ofterdingen*) and the "educational novel" calling for denunciation and sweeping action (Hölderlin's *Hyperion*). The tragic paradox of German classicism was that its very realism signified its defeat, thus encouraging the inclination in Germany to equate flight from reality with victory.

This dilemma is evident in the fact that Wilhelm's apprenticeship, which was still humanly manageable, even playful and enjoyably challenging in many respects, evolved subsequently into the anguished, titanic strivings of Faust to reach the same goal of human wholeness and self-reliance. This is the principal theme of *Faust,* the final, crowning statement of German classicism, which would preoccupy Goethe for most of the remainder of his long life. It neither corresponds precisely to what Schiller meant by naive and sentimental, nor to what Schlegel meant by classical and romantic. At the very heart of this vast dramatic poem, intended to recapitulate the history and destiny of all mankind in that of a single individual, is the contest between Faust and Mephistopheles, a contest between Goethe's human ideal and its negation. Both represent basic aspects or tendencies of humanity which have coexisted throughout history, forming the two poles of all human existence. Together, and only together, do they constitute a true picture of history and its meaning. Where Faust seeks to assert his humanity, to effect that meaningful existence and unity of being for which he longs, unaided by Mephistopheles' magic—as, briefly, in his love for Gretchen and Helen, and in his colonization project toward the end—Mephistopheles remains in the background. Where Faust undergoes self-doubt and defeat, where conditions render him impotent, and above all where he deceives himself and seeks to exceed his mortal limits—as in the episodes of Auerbach's Keller, the Witch's Kitchen, and the conjuring of Helen—there Mephistopheles predominates.

As to the controversial question of who ultimately wins the wager, which, like the poem as a whole, allows for many interpretations, it would seem that neither is the complete victor. True, Faust is "saved," because to no moment of his actual existence does he say, "Linger on, thou art so fair!" which was the condition agreed upon for Mephisto's acquisition of Faust's soul after death. At most Faust says, at the close of his life, that *were* he to live to stand "on free soil with a people free," then to that moment he *could* say, "Linger on . . . ." It is "the rapture of that dream," the vision of a new ideal, represented by the "sentimental" Faust's brief symbolic union with Helen, personification of the classical "naive," that inspires his last line before dying: "This present moment gives me joy supreme."[41] By the same token, however, the fact that Faust does *not* live to see that day, the fact that the workmen, whom Faust believes are draining a swamp at his orders, turn out to be lemurs digging his grave at Mephisto's orders, and, above all, the fact that Faust's redemption takes place in heaven, not on earth, would seem to lend weight to Mephistopheles' position, as expressed just after Faust's death in one of the most provocative passages of the poem:[42]

"A thing is over now!" What does that mean?
The same as if the thing had never been,
yet circles round and round as if it were.
Eternal Emptiness I still prefer.

Although these scanty comments scarcely do justice to one of the great contributions to world literature, even a cursory reading of *Faust* reveals the author's profound insights into both the limitations and possibilities of human history. It draws from the past but faces the future—Germany's, the West's, and that of all modern mankind. For the struggle between Faust and Mephistopheles signifies nothing less than the struggle between the universal forces that can give history meaning—love, self-determination, unity of being—and those which render the human record but a succession of ephemeral events culminating in Eternal Emptiness— obscurantism, oppression, division, and self-seeking, all of which eminently qualify Mephistopheles to be the representative of negation. Either that which is universal in human life, that which makes life worth living for its own sake, must be capable of asserting itself under ever-changing conditions, or else history has no meaning at all. This issue was the crux of *Faust* and of German classicism in general; an issue that came to the fore, not surprisingly, amid the anomie of Germany's transition into the modern world, when there was an especially acute sense that traditional models were gone for good and that new sanctions and supports for humanist values had to be found or that these values might be lost entirely.

Notes to Chapter Two

1. Ernst Cassirer, *The Philosophy of the Enlightenment*, trans. by F. Koelln and J. Pettegrove (Boston: Beacon, 1955), p. vii.
2. Deric Regin, *Freedom and Dignity: The Historical and Philosophical Thought of Schiller* (The Hague: Nijhoff, 1965), p. 90.
3. *Ibid.*, p. 128.
4. Friedrich Schiller, *On the Aesthetic Education of Man*, trans. by R. Snell (New York: Ungar, 1965), pp. 25–27.
5. Immanuel Kant, "Conjectural Beginning of Human History," trans. by E. L. Fackenheim, in *Kant on History*, ed. by L. W. Beck (Indianapolis and New York: Bobbs-Merrill, 1963), p. 63. See also Kant's "Idea for a Universal History from a Cosmopolitan Point of View," trans. by L. W. Beck, in the same volume.
6. Schiller, *op. cit.*, p. 39.
7. *Ibid.*, pp. 50–51.
8. Friedrich Schiller, *Naive and Sentimental Poetry*, trans. by J. A. Elias (New York: Ungar, 1966), p. 176.
9. *Ibid.*, p. 85.
10. *Ibid.*, p. 114.
11. *Ibid.*, p. 96.
12. *Ibid.*, pp. 112–113.
13. *Ibid.*, p. 175.
14. For a searching critique of Schiller's aesthetic theory, see Georg Lukács, *Goethe and His Age*, trans. by R. Anchor (London: Merlin, 1968), Chapters 4 and 5.
15. Schiller, *Naive and Sentimental Poetry*, p. 109.
16. Quoted in E. M. Butler, *The Tyranny of Greece over Germany* (Boston: Beacon, 1958), p. 212. Reprinted by permission.
17. Friedrich Hölderlin, *Hyperion*, trans. by W. R. Trask (New York: Signet, 1965), p. 41.
18. Schiller, *Aesthetic Education*, p. 81.
19. L. N. Tolstoy, *What Is Art?* trans. by A. Maude (Indianapolis and New York: Bobbs-Merrill, 1960), p. 24.
20. For a close examination of the derivation of Schlegel's aesthetic theory from Schiller, see Arthur O. Lovejoy, "Schiller and the Genesis of German Romanticism," in his *Essays in the History of Ideas* (New York: Capricorn, 1960), Chapter 11.
21. Fragment 116, *Athenäum* (1798), quoted in Lovejoy, *op. cit.*, p. 226.
22. Fragment 139, quoted in Lovejoy, *op. cit.*, p. 226.
23. *Naive and Sentimental Poetry*, p. 113.
24. Quoted in Lovejoy, *op. cit.*, p. 218.
25. *Ibid.*, p. 244.
26. *Naive and Sentimental Poetry*, pp. 189–190.
27. Quoted in Lovejoy, *op. cit.*, p. 226.

28. Letter to Goethe, July 2, 1796, in *Correspondence Between Schiller and Goethe*, trans. by D. Schmitz (London: Bell & Sons, 1877), Vol. I, p. 174.
29. Quoted in *Meister der deutschen Kritik, 1730–1830,* ed. by G. F. Hering (Munich: Deutschen Taschenbuch, 1961), p. 208.
30. Quoted in Roy Pascal, *The German Novel* (London: Methuen, 1965), p. 19.
31. Quoted in Pascal, *ibid.,* p. 31.
32. Schiller to Goethe, July 2, 1796, in *Correspondence, op. cit.,* p. 174.
33. *Ibid.,* pp. 175–176.
34. See above, p. 27.
35. Johann Wolfgang von Goethe, *Wilhelm Meister's Apprenticeship,* trans. by T. Carlyle (New York: Collier, 1962), p. 488.
36. Johann Wolfgang von Goethe, *Hermann and Dorothea,* trans. by D. Coogan (New York: Ungar, 1966), p. 93.
37. *Wilhelm Meister's Apprenticeship, op. cit.,* p. 146.
38. Johann Wolfgang von Goethe, *Faust,* trans. by C. E. Passage (Indianapolis and New York: Bobbs-Merrill, 1965), p. 59, lines 1656–1660. Reprinted by permission.
39. *Wilhelm Meister's Apprenticeship, op. cit.,* p. 92.
40. Johann Wolfgang von Goethe, *Torquato Tasso,* trans. by C. E. Passage (New York: Ungar, 1966), p. 16, lines 549–551.
41. *Faust, op. cit.,* p. 393, lines 11,580–11,587.
42. *Ibid.,* p. 394, lines 11,600–11,604.

Sad are we and afraid.
There is no more for us to seek,
The heart is sated, the world is bleak.

Novalis

Romanticism, one of the easiest cultural and intellectual styles to recognize, is at the same time one of the most elusive of definition. This is due largely, at least in the case of German romanticism, to its well-known penchant for obscurantism and multiple meaning, for partial expression and private allusion, and for the ephemeral, the unusual, and the unreal in its choice of subject matter. These and other like characteristics ordinarily associated with German romanticism are most apparent, as already suggested, in the way in which its conception of the nature and function of art in relation to human life differs from that of classicism. Classicism typically seeks to relate the individual to the community in terms of a set of supposedly ideal standards or potentialities common to both. Romanticism conceives art as a means to remove the individual from the community—whether as complete surrender to it, or whether as complete renunciation of it—and to provide him with an alternative source of meaning, identity, or consolation. Whereas artistic subjectivity is one, but only one, element in the larger and more complex picture of reality portrayed by classicism, the subjective dominates and transforms the romantic representation of reality. In contrast to classicism, which seeks to preserve the distinction and interaction between life and art, romanticism, at least in the extreme cases, dissolves this distinction altogether. Where it does not, as in the art of Joseph von Eichendorff, E. T. A. Hoffmann, and Heinrich Heine, life and art are conceived as irreconcilable in principle.

These differences in artistic vision extend to other areas as well. Political romanticism views the state as an organism, a

ROMANTICISM

3

unique homogeneous entity possessing a personality, a life and will of its own, subject only to its own peculiar laws of development. This view contrasts perceptibly with the characteristic Western conception of the state as an ever-changing heterogeneous structure, encompassing a plurality of personalities, institutions, and interest groups bound together by a common set of rights and responsibilities, and seeking to maintain itself in a world of other states similarly organized. Belief in the political personality of the state (*Staatspersönlichkeit*) as a norm for political judgment and action permeates the writings of Novalis, Friedrich Schleiermacher, and Adam Müller, and was later to be perpetuated by such important and influential political thinkers in Germany as Leopold von Ranke, Heinrich von Treitschke, and Friedrich Meinecke. All of them thought of the state as more than merely a historical entity: rather it is the point at which the universal and temporal converge. And the task of politics is to liberate and preserve that which is universal in the state, which means in effect either to purge the state of its

GOTHIC CATHEDRAL SEEN THROUGH RUINS, Carl Gustav Carus
Visual expression of the romantic yearning for a world dead and gone.

(Courtesy, Folkwang Museum, Essen)

THE CASTLE OF THE GRAIL, drawing by Karl F. Schinkel
Romantic attempt to resurrect and exalt the medieval past.

merely historical elements, or else to raise history to the level of the universal.

For history itself in romantic theory is but a glass through which we see darkly the more fundamental metaphysical forces at work in the cosmos. History is an obstacle, a limitation, at best an intermediary standing between us and metaphysical reality. Whereas, for classicism, the eternal manifests itself within, and only within, space and time—these being the necessary conditions for our perception of it—space and time are, for romanticism, fetters which shackle us to the shifting world of appearance. Where classicism seeks the universal within history, romanticism seeks it behind and beyond history. Thus, Novalis' *Christendom and Europe* (1799), quite apart from its simplistic interpretation of the past, which views all of history since the Reformation as but an evil aberration, reads more like an incantation of a mythical Middle Ages than a considered historical analysis or inquiry. Much the same can be said of Friedrich Schlegel's *The Philosophy of History* (1810) and other romantic writings on history.

It is no accident, therefore, that German romanticism found its highest literary expression in the fairy tale and in lyric poetry, which are the least space- and time-bound literary forms; and in the tragedy of fate (*Schicksalstragödie*), which best enables the author to accentuate the illusory and deceptive character of the phenomenal world. Nor is it surprising that romanticism scored its greatest successes in music, the most immediate but also the most abstract of the arts—in the compositions of Carl Maria von Weber, Franz Liszt, Franz Schubert, and later in those of Richard Wagner and Richard Strauss—rather than in literature where only Hoffmann and Heine, among the many gifted German romantic writers, managed to acquire international reputations. Or that romantic painting, the work of Caspar David Friedrich, Moritz von Schwind, and the art of the eccentric Nazarenes drew so heavily on religious and fanciful subject matter, striving more, through the extravagant use of light and color effects, for emotional impact than for visual or mental experience.

In spite of romanticism's complexities, involutedness, and lack of clarity, its intense inwardness and infinite yearning, its spirit of homelessness and loneliness, its obsession with night and death, its uncritical adoration of a mythical medieval past and lamentations and protestations over the supposedly decadent present, it succeeded in becoming the first genuinely popular movement in Germany since the Reformation. Indeed, what enabled romanticism to come to prominence everywhere, not just in Germany, was its instrumentality as a protest against the French Revolution and against the growing *embourgeoisement* of life and art alike that resulted from it. Romanticism's very posture of protest, however, and the iconoclasm and individualism on which its protest was based, were products of the Revolution itself. In this one respect, romanticism proved to be a continuation of the Revolution long after it had spent itself as a political force.

Although romanticism failed to evolve a consistent program of action of its own—in fact, precisely because it failed to do so—it could remain from that day to this the most readily available cultural outlet for discontent, since it possessed the ambiguous advantage of not having to risk defeat or disillusionment. And nowhere more so than in Germany, where fewer alternatives for expressing discontent existed than elsewhere. This factor helps to explain why romanticism sank deeper roots in Germany than elsewhere; why, unlike the West, where romanticism was but one movement among others, appealing usually to the bohemian and outsider, in Germany it became respectable, with many of its leading exponents holding respected and influential positions in society. For, emerging in the wake of a disaster originating from without, which left what little remained of shared traditions and institutions in shambles, romanticism provided Germans, and especially middle-class Germans who would have been the principal beneficiaries of revolution had one occurred in Germany, with an orientation that seemed more appropriate—and more manageable—than any other in an otherwise meaningless and menacing world. Moreover, German romanticism had the cause of national unification to which it could attach itself and broad sectors of the German people. The fact, however, that romanticism, siding in the main with conservatism, succeeded so well in capturing the moral imagination of Germans is to be explained largely by the governing premise of both movements: that of the intrinsic and irremediable imperfectness, incomprehensiveness, and inconclusiveness of all human existence.

Kleist and Romantic Despair

This orientation, or perhaps disorientation, is nowhere more clearly evident or better expressed than in the art of Heinrich von Kleist (1777–1811), one of the few German romantic writers of the first rank and the fiercest opponent of Weimar classicism. His life, like that of so many of the talented of his troubled generation, was beset by failure, frustration, and anguish, ending in suicide at the age of thirty-four. Also like many of them, his exposure to and disillusionment with Kantian philosophy proved to be a turning point in his life and writings. Kant had tried to show that our knowledge of the world is conditioned by space and time, which are not properties of things but are necessary and invariant forms of our perception of things. Space and time, therefore, are not derived from experience; rather they are logically prior to and presupposed by experience. Since our minds thus condition what we seek to know, reason cannot claim or hope to know ultimate reality, i.e., reality unstructured by this operation of the mind. Reason can know reality only as it appears to us within the confines of space and time, which Kant calls the phenomenal world; not as it is in itself, as a noumenon.

As a man still of the Enlightenment, Kant drew the conclusion that even though his theory thus limits reason, this limitation, because it is established by reason itself, should serve to strengthen rather than weaken our confidence in reason. Moreover, by limiting the role of reason to the understanding of experience (the world of appearance), his theory was supposed to discourage reason from making futile excursions into metaphysics, leaving room for faith in these matters. Indeed, faith, according to Kant, although not a substitute for reason or a competitor with it, is rationally possible and even necessary, if restricted, like reason, to its proper sphere. For, Kant believed, if man is subject, like all creatures, to the strict causal laws of nature in that all belong to the phenomenal world, man is unique in that he can, if he chooses, exercise free will, i.e., a self-determining will uninfluenced by the laws of nature. All this, if not typical of the Enlightenment, was at least consistent with its basic credo.

Other conclusions, however, could be drawn from Kant's philosophy. For if appearance and reality are so sharply divided that reality cannot even be known, how could it be said even to exist? Moreover, if man is strictly subject to the causal laws governing the phenomenal world, what could possibly motivate him to act, when occasion demanded, according to self-prescribed moral maxims in defiance of those laws? And how could he do so, even if he wished? Also, how can one be certain that the moral maxims, according to which he decides to act, really can serve, under ever-changing circumstances, as the basis for universal legislation, as Kant's ethical theory prescribes? That is, how can one be certain that his actions, intended to serve the good of all, might not actually result in evil, and that actions motivated by evil might not result in good? Finally, if the world of appearance is knowable only because reason structures it according to its own laws, what is to prevent the conclusion that appearance, too, is not a fact but rather a fancy, a figment of the mind, and not something independent of the faculty by which it is known?

These were some of the questions which distressed students of Kant, many romantics among them. For if his philosophy seemed to rescue reason from scepticism and relativism, enabling it to know with certainty the world of appearance, it did so at the price of denying to it knowledge of reality as a thing in itself. Kleist, in a letter to his fiancée, recorded his reaction to Kant thus:[1]

Consider for yourself, how can we, who are but finite beings and can survey only an infinitely small portion of eternity, our existence on earth, how can we venture to fathom the plan which nature designed for eternity? And if that is impossible, how can a just Deity demand from us that we intervene in this eternal plan, demand this from us who are not even able to form an idea of it?

In another letter to her, he asks:[2]

In truth, when we consider that we require a whole lifetime in order to learn how to live, that even in death we have no notion of heaven's intentions with us, when nobody knows the goal of his life or his destiny, when human reason does not suffice to comprehend itself, the soul, life, and the things around it, when after millennia we still question the existence of right—can God demand responsibility from such creatures? . . . What can it really mean to do evil, as far as the effects are concerned? What is evil? Absolute evil?

Finally, in a casual essay entitled *On the Puppet Theater* (1810), Kleist formulated a thought, derived in part from his reaction to

Kant, which governs not only much of his own writing, but also much of German romantic literature in general. This thought is that only puppets and gods possess *Grazie* (gracefulness, but perhaps suggesting divine grace as well), and that man, because he is earth-bound (willful, conscious, partly knowledgeable), lacks it. *Grazie* is the possession of beings who have either no consciousness at all, or else one that is infinite. Only when men shall "eat of the tree of knowledge once more" will they "fall back into a state of innocence." This will indeed be "the last chapter of the history of the world."[3]

This frankly mystical and apocalyptic vision, according to which man in his present state is but an uncomprehending stumbler in an incomprehensible universe, could not have been more opposed to the classical and idealist conception of man as the ultimate goal and crowning achievement of the cosmos, Prometheus' proud heir. Kleist, in his fast-paced comedy *The Broken Jug* (1807), one of the few successful comic dramas in all of German literature, presents us with the amusing spectacle of a judge, a malicious, lecherous old man, who unwittingly condemns himself of a crime of his own doing while presiding in his own courtroom. Even here, however, we find elements important to his work as a whole: the mindless destructiveness and self-destructiveness of ordinary people, the stupefaction of the parties involved in the face of a thoroughly ridiculous situation, the inability of either reason or feeling to cope with it, an atmosphere of misunderstanding and distrust, the ridiculous masking as righteous and the righteous revealing itself, finally, as ridiculous, and above all the hopeless discrepancy between justice and legality. Underlying this play, as well as his more serious *Schicksalstragödien, Amphitryon* (1807), *Penthesilia* (1808), and the *Prince of Homburg* (1810), are all the questions that Kleist had posed to his fiancée, whom he finally deserted: ". . . when nobody knows the goal of his life or his destiny, when human reason does not suffice to comprehend itself, the soul, life, and the things around it, when after millennia we still question the existence of right—can God demand responsibility from such creatures? . . . What can it really mean to do evil, as far as the effects are concerned? What is evil? Absolute evil?"

To these questions Kleist and his floundering fellow-romantics had no answers. Nor did another equally great writer, Franz Kafka (1883–1925), who later found such great inspiration in Kleist. Both contented themselves with exposing the total inability of man to orient himself in a world in which the traditional sources and sanctions of morality had been discredited and no adequate new ones could be found. On their assumptions, there seemed no viable course but to acquiesce in constituted authority as the sole source of justice men can know in this world—whether, as with Kleist, in the form of brutal Prussian authoritarianism, or, as with Kafka, in that of a hopelessly byzantine Austrian bureaucracy—until such time (whenever and however it might come to pass, and whatever it might mean) men "eat of the tree of knowledge once more." If that unity of being and intelligibility for which men long is by definition unknowable and unattainable, then the world must indeed seem essentially and irredeemably absurd, a theme well suited to gallows humor. By the same token, however, just because man is man, and not a puppet or a god, he is destined to strive for that impossible ideal without which he knows himself to be lost. This was both the dilemma and the challenge of romanticism, but one which romanticism by its very nature was unable to resolve.

Hoffmann and the Art of Damnation

Where Kleist ended his life by entering into a suicide pact with a woman he did not love, Ernst Theodor Amadeus Hoffmann (1776–1822) drank himself to death. Born and raised in Königsberg, a provincial capital that Kant, Hamann, and Herder had earlier helped make an intellectual center of some importance, Hoffmann spent most of his life in the eastern provinces which the Napoleonic Wars had turned into an economic, social, and cultural backwash. There his very considerable talents and ambitions, in law, literature, and music, were fated to go unfulfilled. Even more than Kleist, Hoffmann viewed art as a refuge from the world and a barrier against it; a world he described as "an eternal, inexplicable misunderstanding."[4] His feverish tales are populated by eccentrics and visionaries, criminals and madmen who move in surroundings charged with magic and mystery, the demonic, grotesque, and macabre. His heroes and heroines frequently live and die only for art (like Antonia, in *Antonia's Song,* who literally sings herself to death), and are judged according to whether they succeed in finding their way to art, like Anselmus, in *The Golden Pot* (1813), which ends thus:[5]

"Ah, happy Anselmus, who has cast away the burden of workaday life, who in the love of thy gentle Serpentina fliest in Atlantis! While I, poor I, must soon, nay in a few moments, leave even this fair hall—which itself is far from an estate in Atlantis—and again be transplanted to my garret, where, ensnared among the pettinesses of necessitous existence, my heart and my sight are so bedimmed with a thousand mischiefs, as with thick fog, that the fair Lily will never, never be beheld by me!"

Then Archivist Lindhorst patted me gently on the shoulder, and said: "Soft, soft, my honored friend! Lament not so! Were you not even now in Atlantis? And have you not at least cultivated a pretty little farm of words there, as the poetical possession of your own inner self? And is

(*Courtesy, Schack Gallery, Munich*)

THE POOR POET, Carl Spitzweg
Romantic portrayal of the poet as eccentric and social outcast.

the blessedness of Anselmus anything but a living in poesy? Can anything but poesy reveal itself as the sacred harmony of all beings, as the deepest secret of nature?"

Time and again a pained cry goes up from Hoffmann's stories against a *Biedermeier* world, which provided no inspiration for or appreciation of art (art conceived by Hoffmann as the quest for unconditional truth and an end in itself), and which forces upon men the intolerable alternative of having to choose between life and art. Because the two are, for him, mutually exclusive in this world, the poet finds himself polarized between artistic aspiration and burgher indifference. Left with nothing but his imagination from which to cull subject matter, the poet finds himself estranged from the world altogether. The result is an art that depicts the world as both humorous and horrible at the same time. This we are given to see in one of Hoffmann's finest tales, *The Sandman* (1816), where a man mistakes a mechanical doll for a real woman, falls in love with her, then, under particularly hideous circumstances, promptly goes mad. Like Kleist and many other romantic writers, Hoffmann was fascinated by the deceptiveness of appearance, symbolized so well by the puppet. Only, for Hoffmann, the illusoriness of appearance did not stem from any inevitable limitations on perception per se, but rather from the distortion of perception by the alienated poetic consciousness. Just prior to succumbing to desire for the automaton Olympia, Nathanael can *see* that her eyes are "curiously fixed and dead."[6] It is his desire for her, abetted by the magic binoculars he had acquired from the wrathful, inexplicable Coppola, that deceives his vision. The mechanical doll, far from symbolizing, as it did to Kleist, the ideal of *Grazie*, which is, unfortunately, beyond the reach of mere mortals, becomes for Hoffmann the supreme expression of the alienation of human life in general. Olympia assumes life just when and because Nathanael is being

THE BOY'S MAGIC HORN, Moritz von Schwind
Illustration of the romantic love of youth and pure fancy by one of the most prolific and winsome of German romantic artists.

(*Courtesy, Schack Gallery, Munich*)

deprived of it. And the automaton in this story turns out to be "the bizarre, perverse *Doppelgänger* of true life." [7]

For Kleist, man's plight is the fault of an absurd cosmos for which man is not responsible. For Hoffmann, it is the world's fault for which man can be held responsible. To poetize the world is, in Hoffmann's view, to lose it; to see it for what it is, is to lose oneself. This damnation is the peculiar pathos of his art, an art that was later to inspire such diverse and widely separated writers as Edgar Allan Poe and Nicolai Gogol. Both Kleist and Hoffmann, however, and German romanticism in general, succeeded in posing a dilemma, which came in the wake of the destruction of older, more metaphysically satisfying forms of life and the appearance of newer, less ambitious ones—a dilemma involving the discrepancy between what men now hoped and demanded of the world and what in fact they were able to wrest from it. German romanticism posed the alternative (and threat) of either radical regression or radical progression, finding intolerable only the present tension between unattainable ideals and unacceptable realities. Incapable of resolving this dilemma, it ended on a moral and metaphysical question mark. This question mark, and the aesthetic means appropriate to expressing it, became its legacy to Germany and to modern culture as a whole.

Notes to Chapter Three

1. Letter to Wilhelmine von Zenge, Sept. 15, 1800. Quoted in E. L. Stahl, *Heinrich von Kleist's Dramas* (Oxford: Blackwell, 1961), p. 119.
2. Letter to Wilhelmine von Zenge, Aug. 15, 1801. *Ibid.*, p. 120.
3. *Heinrich von Kleist,* ed. by W. Flemmer (Munich: Goldmann, 1958), Vol. 4, p. 127.
4. Quoted in Ronald Taylor, *Hoffmann* (London: Bowes & Bowes, 1963), p. 68.
5. *Tales of Hoffmann,* ed. by C. Lazare (New York: Wyn, 1946), p. 217.
6. *The Tales of Hoffmann,* ed. and trans. by M. Bullock (New York: Ungar, 1963), p. 21.
7. Taylor, *op. cit.,* p. 87.

The story is a terrible one. It is a fearful thing when the bodies we have created demand of us a soul; but it is a far more dreadful, more terrible, more awful thing when we have created a soul, to hear that soul demanding of us a body, and to behold it pursuing us with this demand.

Heine

Although classicism and romanticism both interacted with idealism, relying heavily at times on the theories of Kant and Fichte, Schelling and Schleiermacher, this interaction did not prevent German idealist philosophy from developing its own distinctive orientation. In agreement with classicism, idealism held that that which is an end in itself—the primacy of man, unity of being, and intelligibility—is realizable by man in time. It denied, however, that either nature or antiquity are the models or means for the realization of these goals. In agreement with romanticism, idealism held that human history, in fact the cosmos as a whole, is activated by the generation and confrontation of polarities. But it denied that these polarities, between thought and feeling, between the individual and society, between the universal and the transitory, are insurmountable in principle, or are surmountable only by appeal to the subjective or to the irrational. Of the three movements, idealism was the one which, initially at least, gave the strongest assent to the French Revolution—Kant, Fichte, and Hegel all looked upon it favorably. While it would be an exaggeration to think of

IDEALISM

idealism as a philosophy of revolution or a revolutionary philosophy, it accepted the reality of revolution more readily than did the other two movements and allowed a greater place for it in its general view of things. If nothing else, the French Revolution taught its idealist supporters in Germany that nothing is absolute and fixed, and that polarities are not forever irresolvable.

Confidence in the power of reason to recognize, relate, and re-solve opposites was the keynote of idealism.

Of the three movements, however, idealism is by far the most complex and foreign at first sight to the non-German layman in philosophy. Both German classicism and romanticism were, after all, but varieties of movements that were international in scope. Therefore, their premises and conclusions were in the main familiar to and shared by their counterparts in other countries. Idealism was a singularly German development and its effects on philosophy elsewhere were belated and marginal. Moreover, the very stagnancy of conditions in Germany served to strengthen the attachment there of the educated classes to intellectual traditions, both ancient and medieval, which had long since been jettisoned in the advanced areas of the West. German philosophy, in keeping both with its deep-rooted Protestant heritage and the German tradition of the university as the interpreter and bastion of truth, aimed from the start to be more than one intellectual discipline among others and more than just a way of explaining things as they are. It purported, rather, to provide an all-encompassing system that would serve to activate men as well as inform them, by presenting a picture both of what might and ought to be, and of what is.

In pursuing this end, German idealism seemed to reverse the usual order of things, or at least the order of things that had come to seem usual in the West since the seventeenth century. There, generally speaking, philosophy held the position that mind and matter are clearly separable realms, or else that the laws governing mind are reducible to those governing matter. It held that things are what they seem to be, since everything in the intellect is first in the senses and our impressions of things are adequate to the things themselves. Following from this, it held that the principal task of philosophy is to explain the facts of everyday experience as fully as possible in the clearest and simplest language possible. By contrast, German idealism held that mind and matter are not neatly divisible, since we possess concepts, like causality, possi-bility, relationship, and others, that do not seem to derive, or to derive only, from experience. Mind, therefore, would not be re-ducible to something else; rather it would itself play a part in ordering the data of experience. If so, appearance and reality may not necessarily be the same thing; for if mind is a distinct but inseparable component of the whole, reality would seem to be something more comprehensive than appearance alone. The basic problems of philosophy, therefore, could not be said either to originate or terminate in everyday experience, and everyday lan-guage would not necessarily be the language most appropriate to philosophy. Hence, the apparent strangeness and difficulty of German idealistic philosophy.

All this in turn implied, however, an even more fundamental contrast between philosophy serving to represent the actual world and philosophy as a means to reconstruct it. Karl Marx would later denounce German idealism in his famous pronouncement: "The philosophers have only *interpreted* the world in various ways; the point, however, is to *change* it." [1] But this pronouncement was itself an extension of the spirit of idealism and its urge to turn thought into an instrument of action and the world into "the sign-manual of the Word" (Heine).

Such an approach to philosophy was well suited to a people for whom almost any alternative was preferable to actuality and for whom almost no alternative to actuality existed but such a philosophy. Had this not been the case, it would be difficult to explain why countless German bureaucrats and army officers, in the early decades of the nineteenth century, approached their labors in a spirit of Kantian dutifulness, since devotion to duty seemed to accord with Kant's equation of the performance of duty with moral freedom. It helps to explain what prompted the perceptive Schlegel to regard the appearance of Fichte's complicated *Theory of Knowledge* as one of the three great events of the 1790's. It helps us to understand why students flocked to the university at Jena, which, before it became a stronghold of idealist philosophy in the 1790's, was known principally as a place for drinking and dueling. We may also understand better why early nineteenth-century Germany seemed to distinguished foreign visitors, like Mme. de Staël, a land of poets and thinkers; and what prompted the far-seeing native son in exile, Heinrich Heine, to declare that the writings of Kant and Fichte "seemed to develop revolutionary forces that only await their time to break forth and fill the world with terror and admiration." [2] Not least, we may understand better why, of those who fought on the barricades and in the streets of Berlin and Vienna in 1848, a disproportionately large number were students and professors, fighting for the advancement of Hegelian freedom. The almost incredible hold that philosophy, and especially such an abstruse philosophy as idealism, had on the moral imagination of Germany's educated was decisively broken only when that fight was lost and Germany, unable to negotiate its transition into the modern world in terms of its own intellectual resources, lapsed once more into disillusionment, pessimism, and reaction.

Kant and the Dominion of Reason

What was there about this philosophy that could produce such effects? There was, in the first place, its postulation of the sovereignty of reason and even its apotheosis. The discovery of Immanuel Kant (1724–1804) that our knowledge, while it applies to the objects of sense experience, does not derive from them, already implied that reason is the master of experience, not its subject. In prescribing its laws to the world of experience, the rational mind gains mastery over that world and reveals itself as a creative power in its own right. Pure knowledge, therefore, or what Kant called synthetic a priori knowledge, is not ultimately a body of concepts about things; rather it is cognizance of the laws of reason on which our knowledge of things depends. On this theory, formulated in Kant's first major philosophical work, *Critique of Pure Reason* (1781), mind and matter are treated as two distinguishable but inseparable elements of a single totality. Pure knowledge is not merely descriptive; it actually becomes a constitutive element of the world of experiences and objects to which it applies. And the principal task of philosophy becomes the recognition and implementation of reason understood as a force that is both universal and necessary.

Another inspirational source of idealism was Kant's teaching, worked out in his second major philosophical work, *Critique of Practical Reason* (1788), that man as a moral being is capable of acting in defiance of the laws of necessity, whether natural or historical, to which he is subject as a physical being. Regardless of the outcome of moral decisions, man is capable of choosing to act in accordance with universally valid moral laws, which reason prescribes to his will. He is capable of so acting because reason prescribes nothing that is impossible or undesirable from the standpoint of the progress of the whole human race. Prescribing these moral laws, which Kant calls categorical imperatives, is the prime function of reason in practical affairs. It applies not only to the individual but to society as a whole. For just as the moral man strives to be free through self-determination, so, too, does the moral society. On this essentially moralistic basis, Kant built his defense of republicanism as the best form of government and his defense of the French Revolution years after both had ceased to be popular causes in Germany.

A theory of morality that emphasized intention over accomplishment, the disposition of the will over the deed, and virtue at the expense of natural gratification was obviously well suited to a society in which any other theory would have been either futile or meaningless. It also raised serious questions, however. For, on Kant's theory, we can at most act "as if" the moral maxims we adopt will become through our efforts universal laws of nature—but we have no guarantee that they will. It was against Kant's position on morality that Schiller wrote in his *Aesthetic Education:* "If Truth is to gain the victory in the struggle with Force, she must first become herself a *force,* and find some *impulse* to champion her in the realm of phenomena; for impulses are the only motive forces in the sensible world."[3] Even worse, if only the intention counts, our moral maxims could just as well result in self-harm or in harm to others, as Kleist attempted to dramatize, in his *Prince of Homburg,* for example. And destruction of persons, even in the name of virtue, actually conflicts with another of Kant's categorical imperatives, namely, that we should always treat humanity, including ourselves, as ends and never as means only. Thus, while Kant's theory had the merit of clarifying the nature and goals of morality and of disassociating it from any ulterior motives, his theory could provide no program for translating morality into practice. If his theory succeeded in giving philosophical expression to a noble conception of virtue, it also reflected the difficulty of making virtue into an effective force in the world.

A third source of idealism's inspirational power stemmed from Kant's aesthetic theory, dealt with in his last major philosophical work, *Critique of Judgment* (1790). The purpose of art, for Kant, is neither decoration, imitation, nor entertainment, although his theory does not preclude any or all of these functions. Art also is not didactic, as the classicists held, nor is it an occasion for unfettered self-expression, as advocated by romanticism. Great art, for Kant, art that arouses in us the feeling of what he calls the beautiful and sublime, is art that creates with a purpose in the same way that nature does, indifferently and without design. "Taste is at bottom a faculty for judging of the sensible illustration of moral ideas."[4] Nature does not work according to purpose, but the artist approaches it as if it did, as if its ultimate goal were a free and rational mankind legislating and acting in accordance with universal moral laws of its own making. Kant's theory of art was, in fact, an extension of his ethical theory, in that both presuppose and aim at the liberation of man from nature (and from history) by reason.

Thus, what is important about art is not so much the product or its effects as it is the process of art, the act of creation itself. Because, in the act of creating, the artist succeeds in overcoming the antithesis between natural and moral man, which Kant thought was basic to all of human history; an antithesis that will be overcome for good and for all only when "art will be strong and perfect enough to become a second nature. This indeed is the ultimate moral end of the human species."[5] Thus, Kant's theory implied yet a third interpretation of the nature and function of art. For the aesthetic here is neither a preparation for politics, as Schiller believed, nor is it a substitute for politics, as the romantics held. In Kant's view, the artist is not only the planner or prophet of a better world—he is its very personification.

Post-Kantian Idealism: Fichte

These theories, and the questions they raised, led to even bolder speculations among Kant's successors. His troublesome distinction between the knowable phenomenal world and the unknowable noumenal world aroused widespread criticism almost immediately. The purpose of this distinction was to deny that things *exist* only as they appear to us within the limits of space and time. Kant held that things only *appear* to us within these limits, a view which convinced him that it is rationally possible and even necessary to assume the existence of "things in themselves," in a state unconditioned by these or any other limits. Due to the limitations of the mind, this state of existence is beyond its comprehension. The critics of this conception, Johann Gottlieb Fichte (1762–1814) chief among them, claimed it a contradiction to assume the existence of something about which nothing by definition can be known. Such an assumption seemed to imply a new form of philosophical fatalism no better than the materialistic determinism it was designed to refute. Both seemed to subjugate man to something over which he has no control. The starting point of Fichte's own philosophy was, therefore, to show that Kant's conception of noumenal reality is an impossible idea. If, he reckoned, the "thing in itself" exists neither beyond nor within the world of appearance, it also, along with all of our other concepts, must originate within the mind. In one bold stroke, Fichte removed ultimate reality from the heavens and relocated it within the self or ego, as he called it. The mountain had come to Mohammed after all. Reality now has no existence independent of the mind which posits it—an idea welcomed by romanticism. Being and thought, appearance and reality, will and idea become but different aspects of the same thing; all are but various phases of consciousness. This insight and its ramifications Fichte works out in his *Theory of Knowledge* (1794) and in his subsequent writings.

Thus, most of the characteristic inclinations of idealist philosophy present in Kant become even more intensified in Fichte. Even more than Kant, Fichte believed in the indivisibility of mind and matter. And where Kant held that the mind can only posit the existence of the noumenal, Fichte went further, claiming that the mind actually produces it. There is nothing known to the ego that is not of its own making, including the noumenal. Hence, for Fichte, even more than for Kant, our understanding of everyday experience depends upon our understanding of the mind that creates it, both as appearance and as reality.

Finally, Fichte believed even more strongly than Kant that the principal purpose of philosophy is to change the world, not merely to interpret it. For, on his theory, reason is the creation and servant of the will, not its master. Therefore, there can be no absolute distinction between pure and practical reason, as Kant had maintained, since all reason is practical in its very origins.

From this standpoint, the world is nothing more or less than the sum of mankind's total activity, the product of its collective ego. Where there is harmony and unity, it is because there is agreement among the various egos that make up the world. Where there is not, this is due to conflict between egos. What unites the various egos is reason. But reason can only prevail if and to the extent that the collective ego wills that it shall. To educate the will to reason and to correct the conditions, social, political, and institutional, that obstruct such education—that is the task of philosophy. And Fichte saw no inconsistency between his calling as a philosopher and his involvement in projects for the educational and political reform of Germany. This attitude brought him into conflict with the authorities at the university of Jena, from which he was dismissed in 1799, and easily could have caused him trouble later in Prussia, where he preached liberal nationalism publicly under the noses of the occupying French forces.

Hegel and History

Georg Wilhelm Friedrich Hegel (1770–1831), in the way in which his philosophy gives expression to the principal characteristics of idealism, and especially in his apotheosis of reason, represents the consummation of idealism. For one thing, he espoused a philosophy more systematic and encyclopedic than that of any of his predecessors. It delves with great originality into practically every area of philosophical inquiry—epistemology, metaphysics, theology, logic, ethics, psychology, science, art, politics, law, and history—and attempts to relate and unify them all in terms of certain basic principles and convictions. Among these was his famous and controversial proposition that what is rational is real and what is real is rational. Another was that reality is the self-realization of reason in time, a process that proceeds dialectically, through the production and resolution of contradictions, until such time as a perfect and lasting synthesis of all essential aspects of the world will have been achieved.

Accordingly, history assumes an importance in Hegel's thinking that it lacked among his predecessors. For instead of being only the story of the past of particular persons or whole peoples, or even the record of mankind collectively, Hegel envisages history as the life-process of reason itself. "The sole thought which philosophy brings to the treatment of history is the simple concept of Reason: that Reason is the law of the world and that, therefore, in world history, things have come about rationally."[6] Reason, which is nothing more or less than "Thought determining itself in absolute freedom,"[7] aims at the "actualization of this Freedom as the final purpose of the world."[8] As history is the "rich product of creative Reason,"[9] and reason, being universal, is ever present and identical with itself at all times, nothing essential is ever lost from history. "The moments which Spirit seems to have left behind, it still possesses in the depths of its present."[10] Hence, to study history as the unfolding of reason in time is thereby to share in and to contribute vitally to the omnipresent spirit of freedom.

This conception did much to inspire serious interest in historical studies in early nineteenth-century Germany and beyond. For it implied that history, despite the catastrophes and setbacks, the injustices and irrationality it entails, is ultimately, even if not obviously, on the side of right. The insight to which philosophy should lead us, Hegel professed, is that "the actual world is as it ought to be, that the truly good, the universal divine Reason is the power capable of actualizing itself."[11] His theory implied further that all history is in reality world history, and that world history, like a living organism, is a single, indivisible unity, an as yet incomplete process which will reveal its full meaning and that of its various phases only at the end. Thus, no matter how dismal and meaningless the past and present may seem at any given time, the future remains open-ended and destined to redeem all that has gone before.

This view could and did serve, therefore, to provide both consolation in the wake of Germany's collapse and hope for the future. What had come to pass was not wholly without purpose, and what could not be made to happen otherwise today, history would see to tomorrow. At the same time, however, Hegel's theory gave forceful expression to the insight that everything human is historical and everything historical deeply and universally human. Whatever good is to be accomplished can only be accomplished within history, and only by and through human effort. "We may affirm without qualification," Hegel writes, "that *nothing good in the world* has been accomplished without passion. . . ."[12] The very essence of spirit is *action*. It makes itself what it essentially is; it is its own product, its own work."[13] Whereas Kant thought of history as "this idiotic course of things human,"[14] Hegel considered it the highest level at which reason is operative, the only medium through which it can arrive at its proper end. In contrast to the skeptical Kant, who always allowed for the possibility that self-destruction may overtake the human race before reason can emerge victorious, the more optimistic Hegel leaned toward the view that the triumph of reason is necessitated and even guaranteed by history.

Finally, where Kant regarded morality as an alternative, a preferable alternative, to history, one which need not and should not heed history in serving virtue, Hegel considered morality as a matter of recognizing and acting upon the potentialities of reason within a particular historical context, no matter how restricted they may seem. "If men are to act," Hegel maintained against Kant's precarious "as if" approach to moral judgment, "they must not only intend the good but must know whether this or that particular course is good." [15] On one thing, however, Kant and Hegel agreed; namely, that the real driving force of actual history, whatever the might-have-been's and should-be's, is the struggle between the rational and the irrational, a struggle painfully evinced by German history, but not by German history alone. This area of agreement amounted to much the same thing. Kant called this struggle the "unsocial sociability of men, i.e., their propensity to enter into society, bound together with a mutual opposition which constantly threatens to break up society." [16] Hegel named it "the *cunning* of reason" which "remains in the background, untouched and un-injured . . . while that through which it develops itself pays the penalty and suffers the loss." [17]

As a mode of self-redefinition in Germany, idealism thus came to fruition in Hegel. Beginning with Kant, it underwent a development whereby reason was first disengaged from actuality, then mobilized against it in the name of general human values, which could not, however, be made to prevail in Germany. Like classicism and romanticism, idealism could serve as an Archimedean point from which to survey and evaluate the overall situation. For that very reason, however, it could do little to change the situation. Indeed, all three movements strained the concept of culture to its utmost limits, denying that its main function is either to reflect, adorn, entertain, or instruct society. Retrospectively, it would seem rather that, in the turmoil of coming to grips with the alien forces of modernization, the most significant contribution made to that process by German culture in general during its great age was the concept of culture as a means of self-redefinition. Since this conception led in Germany almost invariably and inevitably to a culture implying criticism of the established order and a vision of a hu-manly better future, it could scarcely prevail there. And, in order to survive at all under the circumstances, what began in the late decades of the eighteenth century as a culture of self-redefinition evolved by 1815 into a culture of intellectual, moral, and emotional self-containment. Few cultural traditions testify better than the German to the view, as expressed recently by Jean-Paul Sartre, that "culture doesn't save anything or anyone, it doesn't justify. But it's a product of man; he projects himself into it, he recognizes himself in it; that critical mirror offers him his image." [18]

Notes to Chapter Four

1. "Theses on Feuerbach," No. 11, in *Karl Marx and Frederick Engels, Selected Works* (Moscow: Foreign Languages Publishing House, 1955), Vol. II, p. 404.
2. *Religion and Philosophy in Germany*, trans. by J. Snodgrass (Boston: Beacon, 1959), pp. 158–159.
3. *Op. cit.*, p. 48.
4. Immanuel Kant, *Critique of Judgment*, trans. by J. H. Bernard (New York: Hafner, 1951), p. 202.
5. "Conjectural Beginning of Human History," *op. cit.*, p. 63.
6. Georg Wilhelm Friedrich Hegel, *Reason in History*, trans. by R. S. Hartman (Indianapolis and New York: Bobbs-Merrill, 1953), p. 11.
7. *Ibid.*, p. 15.
8. *Ibid.*, p. 24.
9. *Ibid.*, p. 18.
10. *Ibid.*, p. 95.
11. *Ibid.*, p. 47.
12. *Ibid.*, p. 29.
13. *Ibid.*, p. 89.
14. "Idea for a Universal History from a Cosmopolitan Point of View," *op. cit.*, p. 12.
15. Hegel, *op. cit.*, p. 37.
16. "Idea for a Universal History . . . ," *op. cit.*, p. 15.
17. Hegel, *op. cit.*, pp. 43–44.
18. Jean-Paul Sartre, *The Words*, trans. by B. Frechtman (New York: Braziller, 1964), p. 254.

Part Two

RESTORATION AND
THE RETURN
OF REVOLUTION:
1815–1848

*Three elements entered into the life which offered
itself to these children: behind them a past forever
destroyed, still quivering on its ruins with all the
fossils of centuries of absolutism; before them the
aurora of an immense horizon, the first gleams of
the future; and between these two worlds—like the
ocean which separates the Old World from the
New—something vague and floating, a troubled sea
filled with wreckage, traversed from time to time by
some distant sail or some ship trailing thick clouds
of smoke; the present, in a word, which separates
the past from the future, which is neither the one
nor the other, which resembles both, and where one
cannot know whether, at each step, one treads on
living matter or on dead refuse.*

Musset

"From the stagecoach to the railway, the
steamship, and the telegraph, from the faith
of an earlier generation to unconcealed
atheism and materialism, from Goethe to
Heine, from Hegel to Marx, from *Faust* to the
Communist Manifesto—this is a story of
tremendous social and intellectual upheaval."
This is Golo Mann's assessment[1] of the
Restoration in Germany, more commonly
known after 1848 as the *Vormärz*. As the
name suggests, however, the *Vormärz*, despite
the profound changes that occurred within it,
represented both to contemporaries and to
subsequent generations not so much a time of
"tremendous social and intellectual upheaval"
as it did an interlude between two turning
points, a trough between two crests of spiritual
and social ferment. Speaking of Europe as a
whole during this period, the distinguished
French historian, Jacques Droz, writes:[2]

THE *VORMÄRZ*

*Profound as was the economic transformation of
Europe in the first half of the nineteenth century, the
Continent remained essentially as it had been under
the* Ancien Régime. *True, there were considerable
technical advances in industry. . . . However,
between 1815 and 1848 the traditional features of
the economy remained pre-eminent: the superiority
of agriculture over industrial production, the absence*

*of cheap and rapid means of transport, and the
priority given to consumer goods over heavy industry.*

The essentially eclectic and amorphous character of the age was noted also by distinguished contemporaries, whose writings reflect a corresponding sense of exhaustion, ennui, and expectation. Alfred de Musset observes in his *Confessions of a Child of the Century* (1836):[3]

Our age is shapeless. We have failed to stamp the character of our age on our houses, our gardens, or anything else. . . . We have something of every century except of our own. This has never happened before. Eclecticism is our badge: we lay hands on everything we can get hold of: this for the sake of its beauty, that because of its comfortableness, that other because of its antiquity, and yet another thanks to its ugliness; so that we live only on wrecks, as if the end of the world was at hand.

A similar mood of depletion and restlessness pervades Karl Immermann's very popular novel, *The Epigoni* (1836), which tells of the superficiality and anemia of his age, the inability of his generation either to live comfortably with the past or to shape the future, and thus its frivolous habit of slipping chameleonlike "into the pious coat, into the historical coat, into the art coat, and into God knows how many other coats."[4]

Hermann, the hero of Immermann's novel, cannot reconcile himself either to the old political order that was still prevailing in Germany, given a new lease on life by Metternich, nor to the new social forces engendered by the Industrial Revolution, which was just starting to take hold in Central Europe. It is a conflict that dominates the time, and Hermann finds himself caught in the middle. Rejecting his inherited title of nobility, a class he despises for its oppressiveness and lack of *raison d'être*, he reluctantly consents to manage a factory. Unhappy even here, however, he reflects that[5]

Like a hurricane our time rushes towards a sterile mechanism. We cannot stop its course, but neither can we be blamed if for ourselves and our people we hedge off a small area and fortify this island as long as possible against the onrushing waves of industrial development.

In the end, with nowhere else to turn, he withdraws into the solace of idyllic dreams and nihilistic brooding, a pattern that would come to prevail increasingly among artists and intellectuals everywhere in Europe, but especially in Germany, where the tension between old and new remained unresolved longer than elsewhere. To Hermann, to those of his generation who felt that aristocracy and middle class alike were unfit to exist, much less to rule, the present was indeed experienced as little more than that "which

IRON FOUNDRY AT NEUSTADT-EBERSWALDE, Carl Blechen
Illustrates the widespread feeling of grimness and foreboding during Germany's transition to an industrialized society.

separates the past from the future, which is neither the one nor the other, which resembles both, and where one cannot know whether, at each step, one treads on living matter or on dead refuse."

The fact is that the conflict between the old and new, far from being resolved, became even more intense during the *Vormärz*, resulting in an impasse that gave rise in turn to an ethos of stagnancy, despondency, and a sense of loss of the present that pervaded the period. Society's cultural, intellectual, and psychological preference for inwardness, interiority, and insularity; its eclecticism and inability to "stamp the character of its age on its houses, gardens, or anything else," indicated not merely a lack of taste. This lack of taste testified rather to the almost insurmountable task of forming a sense of personal and social identity from elements that coexisted but did not cohere. Under the circumstances, how could German society adhere to or perpetuate the inspired ideals of early classicism, romanticism, and idealism? Without alternatives of its own, however, how could it forsake them altogether? No solution was forthcoming for a generation. Instead, the *Vormärz* remained a limbo, a time of gradual and unsteady reorganization and gathering of forces that would, in 1848, momentarily burst forth and, if nothing else, end the stalemate that threatened to stifle Germany.

This state of affairs was foreshadowed at the very outset by the victory of political reaction throughout Europe. The suppression of liberalism and patriotism, which was even more severe in Germany than elsewhere, resulted in bitter disappointment among those who favored constitutional government and the establishment of a unified German *Reich*. The promises made by German heads of state during the War of Liberation (1813–1815) were recanted in most cases once Napoleon was defeated, and patriots and liberals had little choice but to acquiesce in reaction or else go underground or into exile. Even those states which did grant constitutions— Bavaria, Baden, Weimar, Württemberg, Hanover, Nassau, and Hesse-Darmstadt—did so more to bolster traditional patriarchal government than to replace it.[6]

As in the past universities became a favorite refuge for the disenchanted and dissentient. During the first difficult postwar years, years marked by war weariness, crop failure, economic crisis caused by the flooding of German markets with English goods, a relapse of the feeble middle classes into their former apathy, and the failure of political reform, the spirit of the War of Liberation managed to survive mainly within certain student societies known as *Burschenschaften*. Inspired by the populist nationalism of Ludwig Jahn and by the more humanistic nationalism of the Jena historian Heinrich Luden, the *Burschenschaften* dedicated themselves to the ideals of "freedom, honor, and fatherland" in the hope of becoming nuclei of a new movement for the regeneration of Germany. In 1817, in an effort to publicize their position and gain support for it, they organized a festival at Wartburg to celebrate the third centennial of Luther's posting of his famous theses and the fourth anniversary of the Battle of Leipzig, the battle in which the Allies drove Napoleon from Germany. Metternich and the German princes correctly viewed this event as an attack upon the authoritarian principles and institutions on which their power rested. The following year, however, with the approval of the Grand Duke Charles Augustus of Saxe-Weimar, representatives of fourteen universities met in Jena, a town within his jurisdiction, to draw up a constitution for their organization. But the movement was brought to an abrupt end in 1819, when a fanatical student, Karl Sand, assassinated the reactionary writer August von Kotzebue, who was known to be a paid spy of the Russian czar. This killing, along with an attempt on the life of the head of state of Nassau, presented Metternich with a golden opportunity—"provided by the splendid Sand at the expense of poor Kotzebue," as he cynically put it[7]—to suppress the *Burschenschaften* and to impose the infamous Karlsbad Decrees, which restricted freedom of thought and expression in Germany far more than before.

The concrete effects of the *Burschenschaften* were negligible, therefore, and the role they played in German affairs at this time would scarcely be worth mentioning were it not for what they represented and its more intangible implications. For one thing, these student associations lacked the political education and experience, the power and program necessary to actualize their ideals. Had it not been for the assassination of Kotzebue and the subsequent repression, the *Burschenschaften* would probably have remained a harmless, easily contained student movement. For another, the students, being of a younger generation, were inspired more by the War of Liberation than by the cosmopolitan ideals of the French Revolution. What program they did have, as set forth in their constitution of 1818, was not liberal nationalism in the then ordinarily understood and accepted sense. The *Burschenschaften* advocated a united Christian Germany, but they were against everything foreign, especially the French and Jews. They opposed absolute monarchy, but they also opposed French and English constitutional forms of government that served as models for the newly formed south German constitutional states. At the Wartburg Festival not only were writings by reactionaries burned, but also the liberal Napoleonic Code. The students denounced a hierarchical social structure, but they also rejected capitalism, industrialization, and the "philistine" bourgeois without whose support they could not hope to accomplish anything meaningful. They also objected to the importation of cultural styles from abroad, but they failed to formulate any of their own. Instead, they chose a banner of black, red, and gold, commemorating the glory of ancient imperial Germany, engaged in physical fitness programs prescribed by Jahn, and contented themselves with eccentric dress and behavior.

All of this alienated the *Burschenschaften* not only from conservatives, for whom centralized authority and popular government were anything but desiderata, but from older, more cosmopolitan patriots, liberals, and humanists as well. Of this first German youth movement, Golo Mann has written that "it could not be identified with French or English, or even southern European, political concepts, and did not want to be."[8] Indeed, it was just this uniqueness that accounts for its significance. For the real impact that the *Burschenschaften* had on Germany was to intensify the rift between the educated and society at large, to complicate the conflict between past and present, and to engender one between fathers and sons. Moreover, since everyone else had failed to effect the changes that the vast majority of Germans of all political persuasions longed for, the romantic notion gained impetus that the young, simply because they are young, are better qualified than adults to regenerate society. In suppressing the *Burschenschaften*, the usually shrewd Metternich, who was often more flexible and less fanatical than his opponents and supporters alike, and who was now overreacting out of fear of revolution from whatever quarter, simply succeeded in martyring and giving them a prestige that they would not otherwise have acquired. The student movement's most distinguished and uncompromising leader, Karl Follen (1795–1840), after his expulsion from Germany, emigrated to the United States, where he became a member of the faculty of Harvard University and a leader of the antislavery movement. More important, "practically all the pioneers of German unification grew up under the influence of the *Burschenschaft* and owed to it the pattern of their lives."[9]

The suppression of the *Burschenschaften* was only the occasion, however, for Metternich's more far-reaching measures aimed at the liberal and nationalist movement in Germany, the Karlsbad Decrees. Among other things, they provided for the dismissal of any teacher charged with disseminating "pernicious doctrines hostile to public order or undermining existing political institutions," the supervision of all university lectures by a government official, and a more severe censorship of the press. Jahn was imprisoned; Ernst Moritz Arndt (1769–1860), another inspiration of the student movement, was deprived of his university chair at Bonn; the reformers Stein and Humboldt were forced into retirement along with the well-known journalist Joseph Görres (1776–1848), whose influential periodical, the *Rheinischer Merkur*, was banned; and many other leading figures in German intellectual life were placed under police surveillance. All of this may seem small compared to what has become almost customary in the twentieth century. Compared, however, to similar measures enacted in the eighteenth century, which were often only haphazard and ineffectively enforced, the Karlsbad Decrees were strong stuff indeed and paved the way for worse to come. German intellectuals of the previous generation were often marginal figures in society, but they were usually respected and respectable figures. In the demagogic, nervous Germany of the *Vormärz*, they became almost outcasts or muzzled outlaws.

In 1830, events in France once again rekindled liberal and national sentiment throughout Europe. The July Revolution, an uprising of workers and students that resulted in the overthrow of the last Bourbon king to reign in France, soon spread to Belgium, Poland, Italy, and Germany. Britain itself was on the brink of social upheaval in 1831. In Germany popular pressure was mounting once again in favor of constitutional government. In 1832, at the castle of Hambach, another massive rally was held, this one more radical, more broadly based, and more international in tone than the

Wartburg Festival of 1817. After an unsuccessful liberal *putsch* the following year against the Frankfurt Diet, Metternich's puppet government in Germany, repression set in with renewed force. Hundreds of people received severe prison sentences, and thousands more made their way as refugees to capitals of Western Europe where they carried on their political activity in exile, forming organizations like the *Deutscher Volksverein* in Paris for that purpose. The culmination of reaction came in 1837, when seven distinguished professors at the University of Göttingen—"the Göttingen Seven," as they came to be known—were dismissed for protesting the revocation of the Hanover constitution by the new ruler, Ernst Augustus.

Another source of discontent was the avant-garde literary movement known as Young Germany.[10] Its leaders, Ludolf Wienbarg (1802–1872), Karl Gutzkow (1811–1878), Theodor Mundt (1806–1861), Heinrich Laube (1806–1884), Ludwig Börne (1786–1837), and many other writers more or less loosely associated with them, were mostly men of the artisan and lower middle classes or else Jews. That is, they represented marginal social elements, those most threatened by Germany's self-contradictory state of affairs. In keeping with their class origins, these writers were themselves largely rootless wanderers, without any standing or security in society. Unlike the student movement, they opposed romantic nationalism and anti-Semitism and combated the backlash of political reaction in Germany by appeal to the liberal and cosmopolitan values proclaimed during the French Revolution. They spoke in favor of religious liberty, the establishment of a *Rechtsstaat* based on popular sovereignty, social reform along democratic and Saint-Simonian lines,[11] and the liberalization of sexual mores.

Above all, the writers of Young Germany sought, in opposition to the prevailing *Biedermeier* spirit of disengagement, to press their art directly and actively into the service of their social ideals. Their prime objective was to mobilize and raise the level of German public opinion. As a result, they found themselves, like the earlier "Storm and Stress" writers, sacrificing art to polemics. Not that the two are irreconcilable in principle—Voltaire and Diderot, Lessing, Goethe, and Schiller could be cited as proof to the contrary. In the case of Young Germany, however, both the writers themselves and those they represented felt, and actually were, so threatened from all sides—by the past, the present, and the future—that they found themselves without faith, even an illusory faith, in the possibility of translating their ideals into reality. Without such faith, it was all but impossible to attain to a broad enough perspective, an Archimedean point, that would have enabled them to join art and polemics effectively. Only two writers—and both only on the fringe of the movement—managed to join art and polemics successfully and emerge as the most creative writers of the *Vormärz:* Georg Büchner (1813–1837) and Heinrich Heine (1797–1856), who will be discussed briefly further on. Even then, they were only able to do so by enduring the most excruciating estrangement from society and self. Büchner achieved artistic stature by plunging himself into a total and utter despair that stemmed from his realistic conclusion that the radical, egalitarian ideals to which he adhered so uncompromisingly could not be effected in the Germany of his time; and Heine by emigrating to Paris during the July Revolution, where he found a spiritual homeland capable of sustaining his faith in civilization.

It is not surprising, therefore, that one of the chief characteristics of this otherwise loose association of writers was their ambivalent attitude toward the world and toward themselves. This attitude is apparent throughout their writings; in Karl Immermann's novel *The Epigoni,* referred to above; in Alexander von Ungern-Sternberg's novel *The Strife-Torn* (1832); Laube's novel *Young Europe* (1833); Gutzkow's novel *Blasedow and His Sons* (1838); and in many other of their works. In seeking to set in motion in Germany their ideal of social progress, they came increasingly into conflict with the reality, and, out of sheer frustration at their own inefficacy, with themselves. Thus, paradoxically, and in contrast to similar movements elsewhere, which became central to their country's cultural life, these German writers, seeking to take the lead in social progress in Germany, found themselves condemned by their own countrymen as "un-German"—attacked from the Right as "subversive doctrinaires" and from the Left as "aimless dilettanti." [12] In 1835, the *Deutsche Revue,* edited by Gutzkow, was banned by the Frankfurt Diet, which called upon all German states to [13]

bind themselves to bring the penal and police statutes of their respective areas and the regulations regarding the abuse of the press in their strictest sense to bear against the authors, publishers, printers and disseminators of the writings of the literary group known as Young Germany . . . as also by all lawful means to prevent the dissemination of the writings of this school by booksellers, lending libraries or other means.

A third wave of intellectual ferment, a movement known as the Young Hegelians,[14] began to pass over Germany in the late 1830's. Whereas the student movement had derived from romanticism and Young Germany from classicism, the Young Hegelians took their point of departure from philosophical idealism, in its Hegelian form. As with the leadership of the other two movements, the most prominent of the Young Hegelians, Bruno Bauer (1809–1882), Ludwig Feuerbach (1804–1872), Arnold Ruge (1802–1880), Max Stirner (1806–1856), Moses Hess (1812–1875), and, for a time, Marx and Engels, distinguished themselves more as publicists than as systematic philosophers and were more interested in thought as an instrument of action than as an end in itself. They founded periodicals, therefore, in which to propagate their views, the *Hallische Jahrbücher,* the *Rheinische Zeitung,* and the *Deutsch–Französische Jahrbücher,* all of which, however, were short-lived. And the movement itself effectively dissolved by 1845. Nevertheless, the importance of this development in philosophy was out of all proportion to its immediate influence, longevity, or following. For it proved to be one of the principal conduits through which German thought passed, as in England and France earlier, from its traditionally optimistic, contemplative, spiritualistic phase to one more pessimistic,[15] activist, and materialistic; that is, from the premodern to the modern world of thought.

The basic concern which brought the Young Hegelians into existence in the first place was whether, how, and to what extent the rationalistic foundations of philosophical idealism could be saved in the light of Germany's relapse into reaction and the utilization of Hegel's system to support reaction. Hegel had held that only within the state can the individual become and remain free, and that only as a free being can he be truly rational.[16] Accordingly, he held also that all institutions, including organized religion, should be subordinated to the state. He did not believe, however, that every state does in fact promote and protect the individual's freedom, but only that it will if it recognizes and acts in accordance with this end as its proper function. He also believed that freedom, since it does not derive from any other source, neither from divine nor from natural law, must derive from and be sanctioned by the state. It is true that Hegel regarded the Prussia of his time, of all the German states, as being in the best position, by virtue of its power, prestige, and superior army and bureaucracy, to play this role. And it is no accident that he received an appointment to the University of Berlin in 1818. It is not true, however, that he thought of Prussia as the last word in political excellence.[17] In fact, just before accepting his appointment, he expressed his preference for the new constitutional government of his native Württemberg. Only the political realities of the day induced him to look to Prussia as the guarantor of Germany's well-being. Even then, it was not Hegel, but rather the romantic anti-Hegelian Friedrich Schelling (1775–1854) who later turned out to be the foremost philosophical apologist of Prussianism.

Nevertheless, Hegel's views could and did serve conservative interests. They could be used, for example, to sanction the very foundation of Restoration government, the alliance between throne and altar. They could be used also to sanction the almost indefinite expansion of the state's authority. The theoretical application of Hegel's views to these ends was the work largely of Friedrich Julius

Stahl (1802–1861), a so-called "Right" Hegelian, who used them to espouse a revised version of feudal authoritarian government based on divine right. It was this interpretation of Hegel, and those aspects of his thinking which lent themselves to it, that the Young (or "Left") Hegelians attacked.

The attack was launched by David Friedrich Strauss (1808–1874) in his *Life of Jesus* (1835), a landmark in the scholarly approach to the Bible known as Higher Criticism[18] and a book that became popular immediately. In effect, it asserted the right of reason to interpret all tradition, including religious tradition. And, according to Strauss, reason shows that religious dogmas are not divine truths but rather human myths. The Gospels, for example, although not necessarily untrue, are so illogical and self-contradictory as to be unacceptable as credible historical accounts. The task which Strauss set for himself in his *Life of Jesus* was "to investigate the internal grounds of credibility in relation to each detail given in the Gospels and to test the probability and improbability of their being the production of eye-witnesses, or of competently informed writers."[19] The conclusion toward which he tended was to show that religious beliefs are merely the human (i.e., time-bound) interpretation of truth by a particular community at a given point in history.

Bruno Bauer carried the argument a step further, claiming that reason requires that all religion, including Christianity, be understood historically, as but one phase in mankind's development toward self-consciousness. Christianity, thought of as a strictly historical movement, had long since outlived itself and become a barrier to the progress of the human mind toward freedom. It had emerged in a troubled world in which the human ego grew fearful of itself and "saw the guarantee for its support in the Messiah who merely represented what it itself was in reality, that is, the universal power that it was itself, one in which all feeling for nature, all ties of family, race or state, all forms of art had disappeared."[20] Building on these foundations, Ludwig Feuerbach, in his *The Essence of Christianity* (1841), conceived religion as nothing more than a misguided, injurious expression of the collective psychology of mankind and its own peculiarly human aspirations.[21]

Man—and this is the mystery of religion—projects his nature into objectivity, and then makes himself an object of concern for this new "subject," for this projection of his nature. For God wants man to be good. God asks that man attain perfection and beatitude, for there is no beatitude without perfection. Thus man, while he apparently humiliated himself to the lowest degree, is in truth exalted to the highest; for in and through God, man aims at himself.

Arnold Ruge, who was more influenced by Feuerbach than any of the other Young Hegelians, applied his conclusions to political theory, claiming that what was illusory in religion, the liberation of mankind, could become reality only through political reform. And Moses Hess, the most direct link between the Young Hegelians and Karl Marx, and a full-fledged communist himself, extended the current critique of religion to the social question, which he considered preeminent: "What God is for the theoretical life, money is for the practical life of the inverted world: the alienated power of men, their reified activity." [22]

Owing to their views, Bauer and Feuerbach were dismissed from their university posts at Bonn and Erlangen, respectively, and Ruge, Hess, and Marx never did enter the academic world, all three taking refuge in exile. Although their ideas were provocative in themselves, they became controversial mainly because of their implications. They signified, in effect, an attack upon the actual policies of Frederick William III of Prussia, especially his subordination of religion to state interests; an attack upon the utilization of Hegel's views to support the Hohenzollern regime; and, finally, an attack upon Hegel's belief in the compatibility of religion, philosophy, and politics. Paradoxically, the Young Hegelians, in their effort to vindicate the primacy of reason in Hegel's philosophy, found themselves vitiating the metaphysical foundations upon which he had based it. In this respect, the ambivalent mood of the *Vormärz* manifested itself in the sphere of philosophy also. Still, the seeds of future German thought were sown, as is evident in Feuerbach's position, which was characteristic of the Young Hegelian movement as a whole:[23]

My philosophy of religion is so little a development of Hegel's . . . that it sooner has its origins in an opposition to Hegel and can only be understood in the light of this opposition. . . . Hegel identifies religion with philosophy, I bring out their specific difference; Hegel criticizes religion only in thought, I in its true essence; Hegel objectifies what is subjective, I subjectify what is objective. Hegel opposes the finite to the infinite, the speculative to the empirical, whereas I, precisely because I already find the infinite in the finite and the speculative in the empirical and because the infinite is for me merely the essence of the finite, find also in the speculative mysteries of religion nothing but empirical truths, as, for example, the only truth contained in the "speculative mystery" of the Trinity is that communal life is the only form of life thus not a truth apart, transcendent and supernatural, but a general truth immanent to man, or, in popular terms, a natural truth.

The most significant development of this period, however, was destined to have a greater impact on German affairs than either Metternich or his political, literary, and intellectual opponents. This was the establishment, under Prussian leadership, of the *Zollverein* or customs union. As early as 1818, Prussia abolished all internal trade barriers, and by 1834, most of the other German states, with the notable exception of Austria—"Europe's China," as Ludwig Börne called it—had joined this economic union. Several factors contributed to its success. For one thing, its chief architect, the Prussian minister of finance, Friedrich von Motz (1775–1830), had the foresight to recognize that the unification of all German states into a single tariff and trade association, initiated by Prussia, implied their "eventual unification in one and the same political system . . . under the protection of Prussia."[24] For another, the *Zollverein*, by lowering tariffs and adopting a free-trade policy, gained the support of the all-powerful Junkers, who now had a larger internal market for their agricultural products and a more favorable market for them abroad. In exchange for these goods, Germany received English machines, thus giving impetus to industrialization. Factories, railroads, steamboats, and commercial traffic began to appear where none had existed before. The chemical industry, in which Germany later assumed leadership, also emerged at this time as an offshoot of agricultural growth. In theory, free trade may not have been in the best interests of Germany's infant industries, as the brilliant economist Friedrich List (1789–1846), contended. In practice, however, even without tariff protection, Germany's industry managed to benefit from the other economic advantages provided by the *Zollverein*.

List, an ardent advocate of the *Zollverein* and the industrialization of Germany, fiercely opposed its free trade policy on the grounds, first, that it strengthened the reactionary Junkers at the expense of the rest of the nation, and second, that only an already industrially advanced country like England could benefit from a free world market in which less advanced areas were doomed to become its economic colonies. Such ideas, since they so obviously undermined the political purpose of the *Zollverein*, soon brought him into conflict with the authorities of his native Württemberg, where he was twice imprisoned and then exiled to the United States. There, observing American economic practices, he became even more convinced that nation-building, by means of effective tariff protection of infant industry, was the best course for Germany to follow. This theory he developed after his return to Germany in his influential work *A National System of Political Economy* (1841). Believing that economic progress must promote political progress, which to him, as a south German liberal, meant national unification and the adoption of constitutional government, List argued that free trade for Germany would not only hinder its economic progress in the world, but would also reinforce a semifeudal, authoritarian political system at home. Protectionism, on the other hand, would not only enable Germany eventually to compete favorably with

England in economic development, it would also favor the growth of an enterprising and politically progressive middle class.

These views in turn led List to criticize the source of free-trade theory, Adam Smith's *The Wealth of Nations* (1776), which List claimed was only a rationalization of Britain's position of economic superiority. All economic systems, he concluded, are based on expediency; none, including Smith's, is the expression of eternally valid economic laws. England owed its economic superiority not to the superiority of Smith's principles, but rather to favorable historical circumstances. Different circumstances made it necessary for other countries, like Germany, to pursue their economic interests along different lines. Instead, then, of Smith's view of economic life as an end in itself, independent of the other interests of society and culture—a human as well as a political failing that only England then could afford—List proposed a policy of economic nationalism that would assimilate it to this larger context. Only in this way could Germany prepare itself for a role in world politics and at the same time avoid the evils of excessive materialism.

The significance of List's views, however, went beyond the purely economic realm. For one thing, they testified to the increasing difficulty in general of reconciling liberal and national interests in Germany, a difficulty already apparent in the movements discussed above. List simply gave expression to it in the sphere of economic theory. This dilemma in turn strengthened the tendency among Germans to depart from Western models, such as that of economic and political laissez-faire, in thinking about the modernization of Germany. What choice was there in a society in which an alliance between liberalism and nationalism appeared to be impossible? Increasingly, after 1830, this became the chief problem around which German political and social thought revolved. Leading liberal thinkers, like Karl von Rotteck (1775–1840) and Karl Theodor Welcker (1790–1868), attempted to solve it in the area of political theory, in their *Encyclopedia of Political Science* (1834–1849), by appeal to the idea of a *Rechtsstaat,* which in effect was an attempt to institute modern civil rights within a premodern, antiliberal political order.[25] List, on the other hand, believed that the modernization of society depended upon the modernization of the state. But so long as the conjunction of liberalism and nationalism on the Western model was impossible, so, too, was Germany's modernization along Western lines.

List's most original thoughts went unheeded for the time being, and, frustrated, he died in 1846 by his own hand. Only later did Bismarck make use of them, but then only to adapt them to a new form of autocracy, thus divesting them of their original intent. Nevertheless, the importance of the *Zollverein* is attested by the fact that, after 1840, it became the foundation upon which German national consciousness was built. It was the first practical step toward actual unification and toward the formation of a strong industrial and commercial middle class. Where political theorizing had for centuries failed to achieve these goals, an economic program, which the German people neither initiated nor assented to, succeeded in little more than a decade. In the end, "It was primarily through the material form of free economic enterprise that the traditional political and social structure of Germany began to absorb and acclimatize itself to the dynamism of the advanced western societies." [26]

List was one of the first to realize that economic and technological progress could serve, and in the Germany of his time did serve, to strengthen and stabilize a premodern political and social order. But he was an exception. The actual course of events fostered the illusion among most of his generation that material progress would lead almost automatically to social and political advancement, that it might even substitute or compensate for the latter. This illusion was not confined to Germany, although it came to prevail there more than elsewhere. It even manifested itself in the greatest German literary work of the period, in part two of Goethe's *Faust*, which was being completed just as the *Zollverein* was coming into existence.

All of these developments served to accentuate, during the last years of the *Vormärz*, the basic tension between a traditionalistic political order and the new social and intellectual forces that had emerged in the wake of the French Revolution. As a result of economic growth, Germany's population grew by 38 percent between 1815 and 1845, from 25 million to 34½ million.[27] This population increase in turn posed serious social problems, "providing a labor supply for the factory system, creating land hunger among the peasantry, intensifying the crisis in artisan trades, and driving the masses to large-scale emigration." [28] The advent of capitalism also meant the beginnings of an industrial proletariat. All of these were new sources of discontent aimed at Germany's political order. Protest from all sides grew louder. Middle-class liberals, speaking now for a larger, more productive, and self-confident constituency, protested their exclusion from government and the continuation of a hierarchical social order in which the nobility predominated. Conservatives protested the liberal threat to monarchy and feudalism, religion and tradition, and the decline of the artisan guilds. Some even advocated an alliance between the crown and the proletariat against the liberals.[29] Radicals protested on behalf of the industrial workers exploited by capitalism. In brief, Germany found itself on the path to revolution trod earlier by England and France. Artisans, peasants, and laborers, entrepreneurs and industrialists, all found themselves on a collision course with a political order based on an alliance between throne and altar, supported by Junkers, army officers, and civil servants, and sanctioned by a romantic ideology that looked to the past. In 1848, beset by "the most severe economic crisis since the days of the Continental system,"[30] and prompted once more by the example of France, Germany experienced social revolution for the first time since the Reformation.

Notes to Chapter Five

1. Golo Mann, *The History of Germany Since 1789*, trans. by M. Jackson (New York: Praeger, 1968), p. 52.
2. Jacques Droz, *Europe Between Revolutions, 1815–1848*, trans. by R. Baldick (New York: Harper, 1967), p. 18.
3. Quoted in Mario Praz, "The Victorian Mood: A Reappraisal," in *The Nineteenth-Century World*, ed. G. Métraux and F. Crouzet (New York: Mentor, 1963), p. 29.
4. Quoted in Hermann Boeschenstein, *German Literature of the Nineteenth Century* (London: Arnold, 1969), p. 9.
5. *Ibid.*, p. 10.
6. "In all of them the monarchical principle was explicit. The monarch, of his own free will, invited the participation of other classes of society in the government of the state, but the sovereign still united in his person all the rights of state authority and he administered all the provisions set forth in the constitution." Koppel S. Pinson, Modern Germany, 2nd ed. (New York: Macmillan, 1966, p. 61.
7. Quoted in Kurt F. Reinhardt, *Germany: 2000 Years*, rev. ed. (New York: Ungar, 1961), vol. 2, p. 467.
8. Mann, *op. cit.*, p. 58.
9. Reinhardt, *op. cit.*, p. 466.
10. See Georg Brandes, *Main Currents in Nineteenth-Century Literature*, Vol. 6 (New York: Macmillan, 1906), and J. G. Legge, *Rhyme and Revolution in Germany* (London: Constable, 1918).
11. The appeal of Saint-Simon to these writers was his advocacy of the nonrevolutionary implementation of technological progress within a paternalistic bourgeois political framework. See E. M. Butler, *The Saint-Simonian Religion in Germany* (Cambridge, England: The University Press, 1926).
12. C. P. Magill, "Young Germany: A Revaluation," in *German Studies Presented to L. A. Willoughby* (Oxford: Blackwell, 1952), p. 156.
13. Quoted in Pinson, *op. cit.*, p. 66.
14. See David McLellan, *The Young Hegelians and Karl Marx* (London: Macmillan, 1969); Sidney Hook, *From Hegel to Marx*, 3rd ed. (University of Michigan Press, 1968); Herbert Marcuse, *Reason and Revolution: Hegel and the Rise of Social Theory*, 3rd ed. (Boston: Beacon, 1960), and Karl Löwith, *From Hegel to Nietzsche*, trans. by D. E. Green (London: Constable, 1965).
15. Pessimistic in the sense that it held that the world is not as it ought to be, but not necessarily that it cannot be improved.
16. See above, pp. 55 ff.
17. See Bernard Bourgeois, *La Pensée Politique de Hegel* (Paris: Presses Universitaires de France, 1969).
18. See Karl Barth, *Protestant Thought from Rousseau to Ritschl*, trans. by B. Cozens (New York: Harper, 1952), Chapter 10.
19. Quoted in Sidney Hook, *From Hegel to Marx*, 3rd ed. (Ann Arbor: University of Michigan Press, 1968), p. 82.
20. Quoted in McLellan, *op. cit.*, p. 57.

21. Ludwig Feuerbach, *The Essence of Christianity*, ed. by E. G. Waring and F. W. Strothmann (New York: Ungar, 1965), p. 17.
22. Quoted in McLellan, *op. cit.*, p. 157.
23. *Ibid.*, p. 94.
24. Quoted in Reinhardt, *op. cit.*, p. 514.
25. Leonard Krieger, *The German Idea of Freedom* (Boston: Beacon, 1957), pp. 252 ff.
26. *Ibid.*, pp. 228–229.
27. Theodore S. Hamerow, *Restoration, Revolution, Reaction* (Princeton, N. J.: Princeton University Press, 1958), pp. 19–20.
28. *Ibid.*, p. 20.
29. *Ibid.*, pp. 72 ff.
30. *Ibid.*, p. 76.

Truly the Son of Man is crucified in us all; we all wrestle in bloody agony in our own Gardens of Gethsemane; but not one of us redeems the other with his wounds.

Büchner

Germany of the *Vormärz* experienced a tension between past and future such that, as suggested earlier, many of its creative spirits felt themselves foundering in an impasse between the two. This tension was crucial to the formation of cultural and intellectual outlooks of the time. Its importance is attested by the conflicting social attitudes toward historical time that now began to crystallize in Germany; attitudes analyzed as follows by the noted sociologist Karl Mannheim:[1]

The progressive experiences the present as the beginning of the future, while the conservative regards it simply as the latest point reached by the past. The difference is the more fundamental and radical in that the linear concept of history—which is implied here—is for the conservative something secondary. Primarily, the conservative experiences the past as being one with the present; hence, his concept of history tends to be spatial rather than temporal; it stresses co-existence rather than succession. We may understand this better if we recall that for typically feudal groups (aristocrats and peasants) history is rooted in the soil; the individuals are nothing but passing Spinozistic "modi" of this eternal "substance." . . .

[The conservative and socialist] interpretations of history differ essentially from each other in that the conservative tends to trace history back to organic *entities (of which the family is the prototype), whereas the proletarian sees newer forms of collective entities which are primarily, though not exclusively,* agglomerative *rather than organic in character, i.e., classes, as the motor forces of history. The place occupied by the family and corporation in conservative thought is occupied by classes in socialistic thought; and in the same way, industrial and productive relations take the place of land. . . .*

THE CULTURE OF POLITICAL DESPAIR

6

Thus, conservative thought concentrates upon the past insofar as the past lives on in the present; bourgeois thought, essentially devoted to the present, takes its nourishment from what is new now; and proletarian thought tries to grasp the elements of the future which already exist in the present, by concentrating upon those present factors in which the germs of the future can be seen.

Many of Germany's most creative spirits of the time attempted to resolve this tension in historical perspective by appeal to a variety of attitudes, like utter pessimism, irony and black humor, and utopian optimism, attitudes which tended less to reflect or represent reality accurately than to defy, denounce, or disregard it. Notwithstanding their great differences, what all of these attitudes implied was just this indictment of history; not merely one or another phase or aspect of it, but the historical process as a whole and its claims on the living. Those who expressed these attitudes in their purest and most extreme form were few, but they were among Germany's best talents of the time. They were the ones who effected "the critical transition in sensibility and philosophical outlook" that occurred between Novalis and Schopenhauer; a transition typified, according to one commentator, by the "frustrated romantic who cannot effectively assert himself, cannot completely abandon himself to dream, and cannot abide reality, being tormented by all three possibilities together."[2] He differed from both the earlier "romantic rebel who asserts his own personality, emotions, and will against society out of a sense of injustice or natural genius," and also from the "romantic dreamer who creates a world of imagination in nostalgic substitution for reality."[3] Both of these latter romantic types drew, consciously or not, upon long-standing, deep-rooted religious and philosophical traditions. They still moved, therefore, within the realm of history. The "frustrated romantic," however, was frustrated precisely because in history he could find no inspiration. He was an early form of anti- or ahistorical man. And the appearance of this human type at the highest creative level was the basically new and vital addition to German thought and the culture of the *Vormärz.*

Georg Büchner and *Danton's Death*

The stars are scattered through the night like glistening teardrops; what a terrible grief must be behind the eyes that dropped them.

. . .

We shall have all the clocks in the kingdom destroyed, forbid all calendars, and count off hours

and months with the chronometer of the flowers,
according to times of planting and times of harvest.

Büchner

Although scarcely known in his own time, Büchner succeeded, during his short and tormented life, in becoming Germany's most original playwright since Kleist, and an early forerunner of naturalism and the theater of the absurd. Like Kleist, Hoffman, and other earlier romantic rebels and dreamers, Büchner also emphasized the meaninglessness, misery, and injustice of life—his Lenz (*Lenz,* 1835) calls the universe "an open wound."[4] Unlike them, however, Büchner did not derive his vision from a supposedly unalterable, incomprehensible metaphysical dilemma or from the peculiarities of the artistic temperament. Nor was art, for him, a refuge from life or an alternative to it. On the contrary, Büchner demanded of art "that it be life and the possibility that it might exist—nothing else matters; we then have no need to ask whether it is beautiful or ugly."[5] His art, therefore, could be no more attractive than life itself, which he depicted in the darkest terms possible. He was indeed a "frustrated" romantic, an artist incapable of hurling himself at the world or away from it, lamenting his inability to do either, and finding himself, consequently, a wanderer in the twilight zone between dream and reality.

In fact, Büchner's relationship to the whole of contemporary German culture was strained to the extreme. Idealism in any form he detested, calling it "the most humiliating of insults to human nature."[6] Classicism, as represented especially by Goethe, he admired, but what a strange twist he gave it. Instead of glorifying the triumph of being over nothingness and the fullness and diversity of human existence, he has his Danton (*Danton's Death,* 1835) exclaim: "The pitiable fact is that *I am something!* Creation has spread itself so far that there is nothing empty anymore, multitudes everywhere. This is the suicide of nothingness, creation is its wounds, we its drops of blood, and the world its grave in which it rots."[7] If Büchner categorically denounced existence, he did so on the grounds that it is forever being violated at its lowest, and therefore most universal, level: physical human nature. The principal villain is history, which, far from representing an improvement upon or the liberation of nature, is its destroyer. Once man enters history, and so long as he remains a historical being, he loses control over himself and over existence in general. Only by freeing himself from it, only by abolishing all the clocks and calendars in the kingdom and adopting the "chronometer of the flowers," can he hope to remedy the human condition. But Büchner does not tell whether this liberation from history ever can or will or even should occur, or whether by itself it would suffice to alleviate the emptiness, pain, and futility of life once and for all. In a letter to his fiancée, he expressed his attitude toward history thus:[8]

I have been reading the history of the Revolution. I felt as though crushed by the hideous fatalism of history. I find in human nature a terrifying sameness, in human institutions an irresistible power, bestowed on all and on none. The individual mere foam on the wave, greatness a mere accident, the sovereignty of genius only a puppet-play, a ridiculous struggling against an iron law; to recognize it is our highest achievement, to control it impossible. Never again shall I feel inclined to bow down before the performing horses and the corner-boys of history.

Büchner had much to be bitter about, and his bitterness, which found its way into his art to such great effect, was that of many of the best of his and subsequent generations. Actually, he never really aspired to a literary career; his original intention was to be a successful physician like his father. Once he did turn to literature, his medical studies enabled him to diagnose the human condition in primarily physical, clinically severe terms. While still in school, however, he became involved in radical student politics, which proved to be a turning point in his career.[9] At the age of eighteen he delivered a speech at the Darmstadt secondary school, from which he was graduating, on the younger Cato, an opponent of Caesar, who committed suicide on learning of the enslavement of the Romans. Few of Büchner's listeners could fail to recognize his thinly veiled references to contemporary Germany. In Strassburg, where he went to study medicine in 1831, he became involved in the secret French "Society of the Rights of Man." When he returned to Germany in 1833, he helped to organize a radical student group in Giessen on the Strassburg model. The same year Büchner drew up a declaration of its position, titled *The Hessian Courier*, which was circulated among the peasants of the area in 1834. It was a daring political pamphlet that called for the overthrow of the German ruling classes, the establishment of popular sovereignty, and the implementation of far-reaching social and economic reforms along socialist lines. "Justice in Germany has for centuries been the whore of German princes," it says. "Each step you [the peasants] take toward them must be paved with silver, and every decree paid for by you with poverty and humiliation."[10]

This venture proved disastrous. Many of Büchner's colleagues were frightened by his extremism; copies of the pamphlet were confiscated or voluntarily turned over to the police by the peasants; and, worst of all, a police informer was in their midst, a trusted farmer named Kuhl, who was also responsible for betraying the Frankfurt *putsch* a year earlier. One by one members of the society were arrested, tortured, and imprisoned. Büchner himself, in order to escape arrest, fled the country in 1835 and made his way to Zurich, where he died of typhus two years later at the age of twenty-three. Just prior to his flight, however, he managed to deliver to Karl Gutzkow the manuscript of his recently completed first play, *Danton's Death,* which one commentator calls "undoubtedly the finest first play ever written. It is powerful, relentless, inexorable, passionate, and personal—it is as bitter a philosophical statement as anyone since Sophocles has had the courage to put on a stage."[11]

This extraordinary drama, all of Büchner's writings in fact, represent the experience of a noble but defeated revolutionary spirit transformed into an outlook of total and irremediable despair. As a political activist, the youthful Büchner had badly miscalculated both the revolutionary potential of the downtrodden whom he longed to aid and the strength of the social and political order responsible for their condition. He was not alone in facing this dilemma. Any attempt to provoke revolution at this time in Germany would have met with similar results. Marx himself, as late as 1848 in the *Communist Manifesto,* was speaking on behalf of a social class that scarcely existed in Germany.[12] But whereas Marx at least recognized that the industrial proletariat was the one really potentially revolutionary class of the future, if not of the present, Büchner, in addressing himself to the German peasantry, was dealing with an ultraconservative class that had no interest in or capacity for revolution. It is not surprising, then, that Büchner, betrayed both from within and from without, with absolutely nothing to show for his political effort, would, as an artist, translate his experience into a particularly personal and extreme statement of disillusionment. It was precisely his political involvements and their outcome that deflected him into an artistic career in the first place.

Both elements, however, are ever present and integrally joined in Büchner's writings. On the one hand there is love of life, hatred of asceticism in any form, and a longing for a new and better world in which virtue and happiness would both be possible and no longer mutually exclusive. "Pain is the only sin, and suffering the only vice," Lafotte reflects on the eve of his execution.[13] On the other side are arrayed all the victorious forces of destruction: the transiency and inherent meaninglessness of life, man's inability to control what he creates, and, above all, the mindless, senseless cruelty that men inflict on themselves and on one another. Since the course of events is inevitable, governed by a fatalistic "iron law," there is little room for moral judgment in Büchner's art. Events are judged rather by the tedium that comes from living in a senseless world over which man has no control, and by the dumb suffering that signifies both man's defeat and his protest against defeat. But even if the forces of destruction win out always and everywhere over the forces of life, both elements are equally real and necessary to Büchner's conception of the human condition. For there cannot be a persecutor without a victim. And as surely as his various heroes, the fiery revolutionary Danton, the proletarian half-wit Woyzeck, and the poet-madman Lenz, go down in defeat, what they represent—the protest of outraged humanity—is as indispensable a component in Büchner's overall conception of reality as the forces that destroy them.

Büchner's view of life, therefore, was dismal but honest, dismal *because* honest. The political reality he knew, the German reality, flew in the face of everything he wished to believe, especially his wish to believe *something*. Yet he faced reality uncompromisingly, with all its inexplicabilities and contradictions, and without regard to tradition, convention, or consequences. That is why his art, as disconcerting and unreal as it sometimes seems, is credible—more credible than the simplistic moralizing characteristic of much of earlier Storm and Stress and Young Germany writing, and more credible than much of later naturalist and existentialist writing, where frequently it is difficult to determine what is being destroyed and whether it is of any worth anyway. Frustrated in political involvement, Büchner fulfilled his highest aspiration as an artist: his demand that "art be life." His misfortune was that he succeeded too well. For in faithfully translating his political experience into art, he also implied the futility of political action in general. The result was a damning indictment of life, all the more so as it allowed for no remedy. Thus Büchner was an early landmark in the development of what might be called the culture of political despair; a culture that derives from political experience but does not lead back to it. Its legacy was the awful vision of life, as poignantly voiced, for example, by Lucille, as her husband Camille Desmoulins, is being carted off to the guillotine:[14]

There must be something serious in it somewhere. I must think about that. I'm beginning to understand such things.—Dying—dying—!—But everything has the right to live, everything, this little fly here, that bird. Why not he? The stream of life would stop if even a drop were spilt. The earth would suffer a wound from such a blow.—Everything moves on, clocks tick, bells peal, people run, water flows, and so on and on to—no, it mustn't happen, no, I'll sit on the ground and scream, that all things stop, in fear, that nothing moves. (She sits on the ground, covers her eyes and screams. After a moment she rises.) It doesn't help, nothing at all has changed: the houses, the streets, the wind blowing, the clouds passing—I suppose we must bear it.

Heinrich Heine and the Sorrow of Contradiction

Hear ye not the bells resounding? Kneel down.
They are bringing sacraments to a dying god!

Heine

If Büchner was Germany's least-known great writer of the *Vormärz*, Heine was the only one to achieve worldwide fame. "In the European literature of that quarter of a century which follows the death of Goethe, he was," Matthew Arnold wrote of Heine, "incomparably the most important figure."[15] Despite their different reputations, Büchner and Heine shared something fundamental in common, what one contemporary critic has called an "Enlightenment of lost illusions."[16] For while each sympathized with the Enlightenment and evaluated the present from the standpoint of its ideals, both men, disillusioned with the course of history since Napoleon, discarded its most basic tenet, that of progress, real historical progress. Büchner substituted for it the most rigid anti-historical determinism; Heine the conviction that only art is capable and worthy of guiding life, instead of the Goethean view that life must inspire art. "It is in the hearts of a nation's writers that the image of its future destiny reposes," Heine wrote.[17] And elsewhere.[18]

Mark this, ye proud men of action: ye are nothing but unconscious hodmen of the men of thought who, often in humblest stillness, have appointed you your inevitable task. Maximilian Robespierre was merely the hand of Jean Jacques Rousseau, the bloody hand that drew from the womb of time the body whose soul Rousseau had created.

This "Enlightenment of lost illusions," a romantic defense of pre-romantic ideals, was another form of the culture of political despair. And if Heine was not "an adequate interpreter of the modern world," as Arnold maintained,[19] he was, along with Büchner, at least an adequate symbol of it in its longing for a better human world, one in which beauty and truth would no longer be at odds with each other.

Heine attained his unique reputation because he associated himself, at one time or another during his active life, with every major European movement—classicism, romanticism, idealism, Young Germany, Saint-Simonism, and even communism for a time—but without ever accepting any of them totally or permanently. Almost all of the second half of his life he spent as an expatriate in Paris, where he entered into the main current of European literary and intellectual activity and devoted himself to interpreting and exposing Germany to the rest of the world in several poems and articles. Compared to Heine, most other contemporary German writers of the time were provincial in experience and range of subject matter. Moreover, as a Jew, he was the very symbol of the outsider, which gave him a special perspective on the world, as is evident in these lines from "Hebrew Melodies:"[20]

Long—a thousand years already—
It has boiled in me—dark sorrow!
And Time licks my wounds in passing
As the dog the boils of Job.

Dog, I thank thee for thy spittle—
But it merely cools and soothes me—
Only death can ever heal me,
And, alas: I am immortal!

Heine's friend and ally, the gentile Ludolf Wienbarg, paid Heine the following double-edged compliment, the kind of compliment that could be, and frequently was, used by his many enemies against him and against the Jewish people in general:[21]

No Frenchman, no foreigner, is able to realize and ridicule the follies, the
weaknesses, the pride in ancestors, and the pedantry of the Germans better
than a Jew, born in Germany, who being likewise strange to the heart
and history of the nation has a special bent for satire, which the foreigner
lacks; I mean the stimulus which sprang from the contempt which his
co-religionists had hitherto to endure, the wounded feelings of a nation,
ill-treated through the centuries, and until recently forced to silence.

These qualities, his cosmopolitanism and nonconciliatory individualism, enabled Heine to bring to his art a degree of sophistication and insight, wit and acerbity, that few other German writers of the time could hope to match. These were the weapons he used to attack the hypocrisy and pretentiousness of Germany's religious, cultural, and intellectual life in *A Contribution to the History of Religion and Philosophy in Germany* (1834) and in *The Romantic School* (1836). These weapons he used also to denounce the political and social evils of Germany, in such writings as *Germany, A Winter's Tale* (1844) and in "The Weavers" (1845), one of the fiercest denunciations of social injustice in all of German literature:[22]

Their eyes are dry, for tears are blinding,
They sit at the loom and their teeth are grinding.
We weave thy shroud, O Germany,
We weave a triple curse for thee,
We're weaving and weaving!

A curse to the God to whom we are crying
In the winter's cold and from hunger dying,

We hoped and prayed and implored him in vain,
He fooled us, he teased us, he mocked our pain.
We're weaving and weaving!

A curse to the king who's a rich man's lord,
Who with poor men's misery is merely bored,
Who collects his taxes from hovels and bogs,
And has us shot down in the streets like dogs.
We're weaving and weaving!

A curse to the fatherland which we thought ours,
Where only the vilest corruption flowers,
Where blossoms are scattered before their day,
Where the worm grows fat on rot and decay.
We're weaving and weaving!

The shuttle flies in the creaking loom.
All day and all night we weave thy doom,
We weave thy shroud, Old Germany,
We weave a triple curse for thee.
We're weaving and weaving!

But if Heine was familiar with the bitter side of life, he was also capable of applying his literary talents to its sweeter side, as in his *New Poems* (1844) and *Romanzero* (1851). Justice and injustice, good and evil, beauty and ugliness he judged not from the standpoint of abstract reason, morality, or so-called progress, but by the ability of society to promote human dignity and joy in everyday living. For the expression of this side of life he drew not upon German sources and settings, but from the *joie de vivre* of the Latin peoples and, even more, from a sentimentalized version of ancient Hebrew and ghetto traditions. In his will, written in 1846, Heine expressed his feelings thus: "Farewell you too, German homeland, land of riddles and sorrows, let light prevail, become bright and happy. Farewell, you witty, good Frenchmen, whom I have loved so much. I thank you for your cheerful hospitality."[23]

These two sides of his personality were not unrelated. His critical writings gained body and force from the lyrical and sensual side of his disposition; the latter in turn was steeped in a rigorous sense of moral and intellectual integrity. This duality was but one aspect of what Heine himself described as the struggle between the Greek and Hebrew elements in his nature. It covered a series of tensions that plagued him throughout his life—the tension between the sensual and spiritual, critic and creator, poet and publicist, realist and sentimentalist, citizen and expatriate, German and Jew, fighter for social justice and *bon vivant*. His attitude manifests itself in these lines from "The God Apollo," from his *Romanzero:*[24]

I have been banned from Graecia
A thousand years or longer
But all the time for Graecia
For Graecia I hunger.

All of these tensions imparted verve and appeal to Heine's art. But they also prevented him from taking anything too seriously, including himself, since he sought almost always to defend both terms of these tensions simultaneously. In *Germany, A Winter's Tale,* he reflects: "The stone slips away from Sisyphus, the Danaides' barrel won't ever be filled, and to brighten this earth of ours is the sun's most futile endeavor." His greatness as a man and artist alike lay ultimately in the means by which he sought to resolve these tensions and arrive at a consistent and credible attitude toward himself and the world: the biting irony, mockery, iconoclasm, and unspeakable sadness of an unfulfilled soul. These means of dealing with the world were Heine's principal contribution to the culture of political despair. In "La Mouche," the last poem he wrote before dying, he expressed poignantly, and for the last time, his characteristic view that:[25]

This baleful strife will never, never end
Beauty and truth will always be at variance.
The rift in mankind never will it mend,
Two parties will remain: the Hellenes—the barbarians.

Arthur Schopenhauer and the Primacy of Will

Do we desire to know what men, morally
considered, are worth as a whole and in general, we
have only to consider their fate as a whole and in
general. This is want, wretchedness, affliction,
misery, and death. Eternal justice reigns; if they
were not, as a whole, worthless, their fate, as a
whole, would not be so sad. In this sense we may
say, the world itself is the judgment of the world.

Schopenhauer

Schopenhauer (1788–1860) espoused the culture of political despair from the standpoint of philosophy. All of his writings, and especially his most important work, *The World as Will and Idea* (1819; rev. ed., 1844), from which the above epigraph is taken,[26] assert the deep pessimism, disillusionment, and frustration to be found in Büchner and Heine. Schopenhauer differed from them, however, in at least one significant respect. Whereas Büchner and Heine found the world as it is totally unacceptable from a moral and rational standpoint, and accordingly, denounced, exposed, and protested it, Schopenhauer sought to accommodate his philosophy to it. "Eternal justice reigns; if they [men] were not, as a whole, worthless, their fate, as a whole, would not be so sad." This was not the stuff of earlier German classicism, romanticism, or idealism, although Schopenhauer derived something from all of these sources. Nor is it a thought that either Büchner or Heine ever could have uttered. Schopenhauer differed from these two approximately as Ecclesiastes differs from Job. This was the essentially new note that Schopenhauer sounded in German thought, one destined to have as great an impact on public opinion after 1848 as the philosophy of Hegel, his archenemy, had on it before then.

If few major philosophers have had so little to say about society and politics as Schopenhauer, this is because, as the title of his masterpiece suggests, he did not conceive the world itself to be an objective reality. Rather it is the manifestation of something more primary: the Kantian thing-in-itself. However, Schopenhauer, following Kant's critics, believed that the thing-in-itself, that which is not subject to the limitations of the phenomenal world, must be knowable or it cannot be said to exist. He proceeded, therefore, to posit as the thing-in-itself what he found to be most universal, within the realm of experience, and most immediate to all living things. This, for him, was the will: "Will is the thing-in-itself, the inner content, the essence of the world. Life, the visible world, the phenomenon, is only the mirror of the will."[27] Or, again: "The world is just what it is, because the will, whose manifestation it is, is what it is, because it so wills."[28]

Even if it were true, however, that the will is that which is most fundamental to life, and the *sine qua non* of the world's existence, it does not necessarily follow that the will qualifies as a noumenon in the Kantian sense. It could very well be, as Kant himself recognized, only another aspect, however significant, of the phenomenal world, one subject to all its limitations and governance. Schopenhauer's equation of the will with noumenal reality, like Kant's own claim that such a reality exists but is *ipso facto* unknowable, was only an unproved and unprovable assumption. This assumption, which he sustained more by brilliant rhetoric than by careful reasoning, was momentous, however. For it implied both that philosophy need not concern itself particularly with the world as such, since the world is nothing more than a manifestation of the will anyway, and that the will could claim primacy over intellect. This was the starting point of a philosophy whose influence on German thought and opinion in the nineteenth century was second to none.

But Schopenhauer not only reversed the order of will and intellect in Western (and German) thought thus far; he also denied their harmonious interdependence. His will is a blind, insatiable force, the purely egoistic impulse to survive no matter what. It works toward no rational, universal end and makes use of the intellect only to justify and rationalize its self-seeking acts. "In fact, freedom from all aim, from all limits, belongs to the nature of the will, which is an endless striving." [29] But since the will is an "endless striving," since "every satisfied wish at once makes room for a new one," [30] life must always, or nearly always, end in tragedy. "The subject of willing is constantly stretched on the revolving wheel of Ixion, pours water into the sieve of the Danaides, is the ever-longing Tantalus." [31] The only escape from this dilemma, one reserved for a disciplined few, is the negation of the will by means of art. Only the arts, according to Schopenhauer, because they deal with what is timeless and unchanging, with pure ideas in the Platonic sense, can console man and distract him from the vicissitudes of existence. The contemplation of art enables man to divest himself of his individuality and to enter into the realm of universals. Pure science and philosophy perform the same function. Schopenhauer, one of the first modern philosophers to begin to take non-Western thought seriously, found support for his view in Buddhism and its teaching of the way to Nirvana through denial of the self and the world. In seeking support in this direction, he was also giving voice to the then novel notion that Western traditions of thought in general were inadequate to meet the basic spiritual needs of modern man.

The world as will and the world as idea, the two are forever irreconcilable in Schopenhauer's theory. True, he failed to explain what could prompt a few special individuals at any given time to suppress their wills and seek redemption in the passive contemplation of art or in pure thought. To have done so, to have argued that the will may not be primary, or that it may not be by nature totally irrational, or that it may on occasion be influenced by the intellect, would have jeopardized his whole theory. For, in Schopenhauer's own view, the validity of his theory depended upon its ability to explain, in a philosophically satisfactory manner, the pain of existence—the centrality, the inevitability, and the justification of pain to all life.

From the standpoint of the history of German thought, however, Schopenhauer's defects in reasoning were far less important than his departure from earlier German intellectual currents. No longer is genius but the normal man fully developed, the poet and man of action combined, as with Goethe. For Schopenhauer, "The difference between the genius and the ordinary man, no doubt, is a *quantitative* one, insofar as it is a difference of degree; but I am tempted to regard it also as *qualitative,* in view of the fact that ordinary minds, notwithstanding individual variation, have a certain tendency to think alike." [32] No longer is art the handmaiden of reason, as with Schiller. No longer is the function of philosophy to understand the phenomenal world according to the laws of reason, as with Kant. Schopenhauer was not even a romantic in the traditional sense. He did not advocate the assertion or fulfillment of personality for its own sake, or attack the world out of a sense of outraged genius, or seek to substitute fantasy for reality. A new motif appeared in Schopenhauer that was destined to come to the fore of German romanticism thereafter: the association of the creative act with death and destruction. Traditional humanism emerges in his theory as sterile and effete, a means of self-annihilation. Man must deny himself to save himself; he must die to the world to be born to a state of spiritual quiescence. Thus, while Schopenhauer placed a high value on creativity and learning, they did not represent to him a crowning achievement of mankind collectively or an indispensable path to enlightenment and progress. Rather, they provided, to a solitary few, the most effective refuge and distraction from the self and the world. "Knowledge . . . affords the possibility of the suppression of willing, of salvation through freedom, of conquest and annihilation of the world."[33]

To none, understandably, was Schopenhauer more opposed than to Hegel, his philosophical antithesis in every essential respect.[34] Life and mind, reason and reality are so intertwined in Hegel as to be inseparable. In Schopenhauer, they never meet. For Hegel, nothing is too trivial or isolated not to play some role in the larger scheme of things. Since no larger scheme of things existed for Schopenhauer, nothing, not even the apparently momentous, can have any true significance. And, whereas Hegel considered history, since it is nothing less than the unfolding of reason in time effected by and through human agents, as the most comprehensive and meaningful way to understand human reality, Schopenhauer regarded it as "the favorite study of those who wish to learn something, without having to face the effort demanded by any branch of real knowledge, which taxes the intelligence."[35]

History, for Schopenhauer, was little more than an irrational sequence of evanescent events, which may be "interesting" but not really important from the standpoint of philosophy. This view was logical for a thinker who had little regard for understanding of the self in relation to the world or of the world conceived as a coherent, intrinsically meaningful process. Whatever the defects of Hegel's theory of history, and however salutary Schopenhauer's criticism of it in the name of that which cannot be fitted neatly into abstractly rational terms, his own puckish, sweeping generalizations about the world are such that history can neither prove nor disprove them. What could history possibly mean to a man who held that "to those in whom the will has turned and denied itself, this our world, which is so real, with all its suns and milky-ways, is nothing"?[36] Schopenhauer's philosophy was the most extreme expression to date of the culture of political despair and proved to be its chief legacy to educated Germans in the second half of the century, including such leading figures as Richard Wagner and Friedrich Nietzsche, Theodor Fontane and Thomas Mann.

The Early Marx and the German Question

In direct contrast to German philosophy, which
descends from heaven to earth, here we ascend from
earth to heaven.

Marx

At first sight it might seem out of order to classify Karl Marx (1818–1883), and especially Marx after 1848, as representative of a distinctively German culture of political despair. Throughout his life he combated, in his own way, everything in social and political theory and in literature and philosophy that he considered to be cynical or defeatist, obscurantist or irresolute. Moreover, as a thoroughgoing radical, he had supreme confidence in the future, a confidence that few but confirmed radicals have ever been able to share.[37] The prophetic and optimistic aspects of his doctrine, as embodied in his absolute belief in the possibility, indeed the inevitability, of a drastically improved future society, are well known. And after fleeing Germany in 1843, Marx became more concerned with European and global developments than with specifically German events. He was the founder of an international revolutionary movement which has always had little regard (often to its detriment) for specifically national traditions and characteristics. And the fact that communism never came to power in a united Germany, the fact that official Germany subsequently always worked to suppress it, simply attests to how little the success of Marx's doctrines depended upon what happened there.

However, all of this ought not to obscure how greatly, especially before 1848, Marx's thought was shaped by his German experience. Until then, most of his writings—his articles for the *Rheinische Zeitung* and the *Deutsch–Französische Jahrbücher* in 1843–1844, and his works, *The Holy Family* (1845) and *The German Ideology* (1845–1846), written in collaboration with his life-long friend and associate, Friedrich Engels (1820–1895)—were concerned chiefly with German affairs. In this formative phase of his career, he began to develop his views on the larger issues in the process of defining his position vis-à-vis Germany: the two went hand in hand during this time. Even after 1848, his views on history and society in general would still bear some of the traces of their Germanic origin. For example, in contrast to Marx's own wishes and expectations,

KARL MARX
This photograph captures the stern and uncompromising
quality of the great man of socialism.

communism has always had least success in the already industrially
advanced countries. It has been most successful in countries that
most resembled Germany of the midnineteenth century: countries
in transition from an agrarian to an industrial economy but still
lacking strong working-class movements with socialist aims. The
national peculiarities of German socialist thought in general, and
of German Marxism in particular, are evident also in their speculative, apocalyptic, and dogmatic qualities, in contrast to the more
pragmatic and practical character of socialism in France and England. One reason for these qualities was that German socialism,
again in contrast to socialism elsewhere, was the creation of an
intellectual elite in a country where it initially lacked mass support.
If Marx's ideas fell on deaf ears in 1848, this was because they
came too late to have any appreciable impact on the advanced
countries of Western Europe, and too early to influence German
affairs. Thereafter, however, the German socialist movement, which
soon assumed leadership of the European socialist movement as a
whole until 1914, became more markedly Marxist, even in its "revisionist" phase, than any of the other European socialist movements.

There is justification, therefore, for thinking of the early Marx as a major interpreter of the Germany of his time. Judging from his writings of the 1840's, there is justification also for thinking of him as an original contributor to the culture of political despair as it was then emerging in Germany. True, Marx was far removed from the pessimism and sense of the world's meaninglessness to be found in Büchner and Schopenhauer. And, although he and Heine were friends and collaborators for a time in Paris, even Heine found himself retreating from a position which held that the oppressed proletariat, just because it is oppressed by an inhuman capitalist ruling class, is entitled and destined to be the savior of all mankind once and for all; and that salvation will entail the obliteration of history and society as it will have developed up to that momentous event. As early as the 1830's, years before Marx appeared on the scene, Heine had warned against the revolutionary implications of earlier German philosophy:[38]

Then will appear Kantians as little tolerant of piety in the world of deeds as in the world of ideas, who will mercilessly upturn with sword and axe the soil of our European life in order to extirpate the last remnants of the past. There will come upon the scene armed Fichteans whose fanaticism of will is to be restrained neither by fear nor by self-interest; for they live in the spirit; they defy matter like those early Christians who could be subdued neither by bodily torments nor by bodily delights.

Marx, although a severe critic of earlier German idealism, especially in its Hegelian and post-Hegelian forms, nevertheless retained and elaborated its revolutionary spirit. As early as 1844, in his *Critique of Hegel's Philosophy of Right*, he stated his position on the role of the proletariat in history, thus:[39]

Where, then, is the positive *possibility of a German emancipation?*
Answer: In the formation of a class with radical chains, *a class of civil society which is not a class of civil society, an estate which is the dissolution of all estates, a sphere which has a universal character by its universal suffering and claims no* particular right *because no* particular wrong *but* wrong generally *is perpetrated against it; which can invoke no* historical *but only its* human *title, which does not stand in any one-sided opposition to the consequences but in all-round opposition to the presuppositions of the German political system; a sphere, finally, which cannot emancipate itself without emancipating itself from all other spheres of society, and thereby emancipating all other spheres of society, which, in a word, is the* complete loss *of man, and hence can win itself only through the* complete re-winning of man. *This dissolution of society as a particular estate is the* proletariat. . . .

By heralding the dissolution of the hereto existing world order *the proletariat merely proclaims the* secret of its own existence, *for it is the* actual *dissolution of that world order.*

This characteristic statement reveals to what extent Marx's main ideas derived from his interpretation of German society. Although he was addressing himself to modern society as a whole, Germany served as a model in his early thinking. Germany embodied, in a more extreme and degrading form than any other country, all the essential traits that Marx came to associate with modern society at large: the dehumanization of man by the retention of precapitalist and the introduction of capitalist modes of production, and by a political system and culture that served their interests. Precisely because Germany was a microcosm of modern society in its worst form, nothing short of sweeping revolution could improve it. "In Germany *no* kind of bondage can be shattered without *every* kind of bondage being shattered. The *fundamental* Germany cannot revolutionize without revolutionizing *from the foundation.*" [40] This evaluation allowed Marx to argue that *"the emancipation of the German is the emancipation of man."* [41] In brief, Marx's thoroughgoing optimism about the future emancipation of mankind, with Germany in the forefront, rested on his equally thoroughgoing pessimism with respect to the past and present, as exemplified especially by German history.

This viewpoint implied another, even more radical, sense in which Marx contributed to the culture of political despair. For, compared to Marxism, all previous German intellectual traditions were, in at least one important respect, essentially conservative, as Marx himself recognized. Classicism, romanticism, and idealism, whatever their differences, all found some value in the past and incorporated into their respective world views some degree of dependency on the past. In his portrayal of the proletariat, cited above, Marx was not merely crying out against the injustices suffered by this exploited class and defending it solely on moral grounds. Rather, he assigned to it the role of liberator of mankind precisely because it is the one class "which can invoke no *historical* but only its *human* title"; a class, therefore, which represents "the *complete loss* of man, and hence can win itself only through the *complete re-winning of man."* On Marx's theory—and this is in part what differentiates it from what he and Engels contemptuously called "utopian" socialism—the proletariat does not merely *proclaim* "the dissolution of the hereto existing world order"; it actually *personifies* it. The very existence of such a social class, dispossessed of its historical title, but still, and for that very reason, in possession of its human title, provided sufficient grounds for Marx to indict the historical process as a whole. In support of his views, he appealed to the humanistic, dialectical, and iconoclastic side of earlier German thought, but only to denounce its traditionalism and irrelevance to the realities of the modern world, as they appeared to him. In adopting this stance he simply carried to its logical extreme the tension between past and future characteristic of the culture of the *Vormärz* in general: the two are almost mutually exclusive in Marx. So far as Germany was concerned, not the least significance of Marx's early writings was precisely that they gave forceful expression to, and helped shape, a desperate decision that was already in the offing there: the choice between a futureless past and a pastless future.

1848: The German Revolution and Its Significance

A revolution is a misfortune, but an even greater
misfortune is a revolution that fails.

Heine

The revolutions that took place in Vienna and Berlin in March 1848 were but part of the larger pattern of upheaval that extended from Scandinavia to southern Italy and from France to Central Europe.[42] Had revolution not broken out again in Paris, the city acknowledged throughout Europe as the center and symbol of revolution since 1789, almost certainly revolution would not have occurred in Germany. For the first time in their history, Germans sought to solve their political and social problems by liberal and democratic means implemented by popular action against autocratic authority. At that moment, until the swift and ignominious defeat of its revolution and the restoration of reaction, Germany found itself more in accord with the main lines of development in the West than ever before or since.

For that very reason the stakes of revolution were higher in Germany than elsewhere. Germany was not only fighting for political birth in the form of a unified national state; it was also fighting for the victory of the centrifugal and universalistic over the centripetal, particularistic aspects of its historical existence and traditions. Liberalism and democracy, nationalism and internationalism—these were the causes for which the revolutionaries throughout Europe fought in 1848. Owing to the growing preponderance of the divisive, hierarchical forces in European affairs during the Restoration, these causes were, moreover, almost the only bonds in terms of which the different peoples could relate to one another. The victory of revolution in Europe at large could have provided the basis for a new European unity, one no longer dependent on the primacy of any particular geographical region,

STREET FIGHT IN BERLIN, MARCH 1848
A record of the storming of the Berlin arsenal.

national tradition, or hitherto existing set of historical circumstances. The victory of revolution in Germany could have demonstrated that modernization is not necessarily equivalent to or dependent upon westernization, and that differing historical traditions
can be adapted to similar ends.

As it turned out, the revolutionary effort failed almost everywhere. The rifts, both real and imaginary, between the West and
the rest of the world widened, and the equation of the West with
the modern became more firmly entrenched in the minds of men
throughout Europe. To accept one was to accept the other, and to
reject either was to reject both. This line of thought manifested
itself in the growth, during the second half of the century, in Central
and Eastern Europe and in other non-Western areas of the world,
of the various "pan" movements, like pan-Germanism and pan-
Slavism, which stood in opposition to local westernizing movements. Another result was the growth of such dichotomies in intellectual life as that between Spirit and Life (Nietzsche and Thomas
Mann), Community and Society (Lagarde and Tönnies), Culture and
Civilization (Burckhardt and Spengler)—the first term in each case
designating that which is indigenous, native, authentic, and the
second signifying that which is alien, Western, and hostile. Revolution in 1848 tested liberal traditions everywhere; in Germany it

exhausted them. The German revolutionaries had found inspiration in their pre-Restoration heritage—in those aspects of classicism, romanticism, and idealism which lent themselves to political liberalism and cultural humanism. The failure of revolution marked the decline of this heritage as a vital element in German affairs. The culture of political despair, which had only been peripheral before 1848, came rapidly to the fore thereafter. Schopenhauer displaced Hegel as Germany's leading philosophical light. The natural sciences began to outshine the humanistic disciplines in German higher education. And only after 1848 did German literary criticism begin, for the first time, to characterize Goethe as an "Olympian," that is, as a talent to be admired from afar, but not to be simulated or assimilated to everyday life, since, as a "god," he was now beyond the merely human reach.

Thus, 1848 signalized the failure of Germany to enter into the modern world on the basis of its own best historical resources. True, in the second half of the century, Germany rapidly adapted in externals to the dynamism of the advanced Western countries, but only at the cost of repudiating or drastically revising its own self-image. In Germany, as elsewhere, modernization did, for better or worse, come in the form of westernization. Not surprisingly, the debtor came to harbor a highly ambivalent attitude toward the creditor: hatred and contempt mixed with respect and admiration. This attitude took the form in Germany of rebuilding an internal self designed to counteract the effects of historical dislocation, a development to be repeated subsequently with variations in other parts of the world. This development, set in motion by the events of 1848, would impart to German thought and culture its characteristic tone until well into the twentieth century. Thus did Germany arrive at the midcentury mark.

Notes to Chapter Six

1. From "Conservative Thought," in *Essays on Sociology and Social Psychology*, ed. by P. Kecskemeti (1953), pp. 111–113. Reprinted by permission of Oxford University Press and Routledge & Kegan Paul.
2. Ronald Peacock, "Novalis and Schopenhauer. A Critical Transition in Romanticism," in *German Studies Presented to L. A. Willoughby* (Oxford: Blackwell, 1952), p. 143.
3. *Loc. cit.*
4. Georg Büchner, *Complete Plays and Prose*, trans. by C. R. Mueller (New York: Hill and Wang, 1963), p. 148.
5. *Ibid.*, p. 150.
6. *Loc. cit.*
7. *Ibid.*, p. 56.
8. Quoted in J. P. Stern, *Re-interpretations: Seven Studies in Nineteenth-Century German Literature* (New York: Basic Books, 1964), p. 95.

9. For Büchner's political activities, see Willi Sternfeld, "German Students and Their Professors," in *In Tyrannos: Four Centuries of Struggle Against Tyranny in Germany*, ed. by H. J. Rehfisch (London: Drummond, 1944), pp. 133 ff.
10. Büchner, *op. cit.*, p. 171.
11. *Ibid.*, p. xii.
12. For the irrelevance of Marx to the 1848 revolutions in Germany, see Theodore S. Hamerow, *op. cit.*, pp. 67 ff.
13. Büchner, *op. cit.*, p. 51.
14. *Ibid.*, p. 70.
15. Quoted in *Heine: Prose and Poetry*, ed. by Ernest Rhys (New York: Dutton, 1966), p. xv.
16. Hans Mayer, *Von Lessing bis Thomas Mann* (Metzingen/Württemberg: Neske, 1959), p. 284.
17. Quoted in Kurt Weinberg, *Henri Heine: "Romantique Defroqué"* (Paris: Presses Universitaires de France, 1954), p. 135.
18. *Religion and Philosophy in Germany*, trans. by J. Snodgrass (Boston: Beacon, 1959), p. 106.
19. Quoted in *Heine: Prose and Poetry, op. cit.*, p. xv.
20. As found in *Heine: Prose and Poetry*, p. 144. This selection translated by Margaret Armour, Everyman's Library edition. Published by E. P. Dutton & Co., Inc. and J. M. Dent & Sons Ltd and used with their permission.
21. Quoted in Ernest K. Bramsted, *Aristocracy and the Middle Classes in Germany: Social Types in German Literature, 1830–1900.* rev. ed. (Chicago and London: Phoenix Books, 1964), pp. 302–303.
22. As found in *Heine* by Meno Spann (London: Bowes & Bowes, 1966), pp. 63–64. Reprinted by permission.
23. Quoted in Hermann Boeschenstein, *op. cit.*, p. 56.
24. Spann, *op. cit.*, p. 76.
25. *Ibid.*, p. 88.
26. *The Philosophy of Schopenhauer*, ed. by I. Edman (New York: Modern Library, 1928), p. 281.
27. *Ibid.*, p. 217.
28. *Ibid.*, p. 275.
29. *Ibid.*, p. 133.
30. *Ibid.*, p. 162.
31. *Loc. cit.*
32. Arthur Schopenhauer, *The Art of Literature, Selections from Parerga and Paralipomena*, trans. by T. B. Saunders (Ann Arbor: University of Michigan Press, 1960), p. 100.
33. *The Philosophy of Schopenhauer, op. cit.*, p. 274.
34. For Schopenhauer's view of Hegel, see the preface to the first edition of his *On the Basis of Morality*, trans. by E. F. J. Payne (Indianapolis: Bobbs-Merrill, 1965), pp. 3 ff.
35. *The Art of Literature, op. cit.*, p. 58.
36. *The Philosophy of Schopenhauer, op. cit.*, p. 335.
37. See Mannheim's sociological characterization of radical thought above, pp. 77–78.
38. Heine, *Religion and Philosophy in Germany, op. cit.*, p. 159.
39. Quoted in *Marx and Engels: Basic Writings on Politics and Philosophy*, ed. by L. S. Feuer (New York: Doubleday, 1959), pp. 264–265.
40. *Ibid.*, p. 266.
41. *Loc. cit.*
42. For an overview of the 1848 revolutions, see *The Opening of an Era: 1848*, ed. by F. Fejtö (London: Wingate, 1948), and *1848: A Turning Point?*, ed. by M. Kranzberg (Boston: Heath, 1959), which contains an extensive bibliography.

Part Three

TOWARD UNIFICATION AND CONSOLIDATION: 1850–1890

The time of ideals is past. German unity has come down from the world of dreams into the prosaic world of reality. Today, more than ever, politicians must ask not what is desirable, but what is attainable.

Johannes Miquel

The biggest change that came over German public life after midcentury was the memory and aftermath of an unsuccessful revolution aimed at the creation of a unified, popular state. Under other circumstances, the demoralization that set in among those who had supported these liberal goals might not have been so great. But Germany, unlike England and France, had not experienced social upheaval since the Reformation, and therefore lacked a progressive tradition capable of sustaining or counteracting a major setback. Thus, the events of 1848 and 1849 were bound to have far-reaching effects, and not only on liberals, but on Germans of all political and ideological persuasions. For it was rapidly becoming apparent to all that, regardless of the desirability of these goals, they might not be attainable by any means, at least not as a single, interdependent program, as envisaged hitherto by German and Western liberals alike. Once the proposition was accepted that a strong, unified state and popular government need not go hand in hand, that one could very well come into being without or at the expense of the other—and, given the conditions of Germany at this time, it was inevitable that *Einheit* would take precedence over *Freiheit*—the back of German liberalism was broken.

This turn of events served to remove Germany farther than ever from both the advanced West and its own best traditions. For without the common bond of liberal, humanist ideals, Germany had little with which to relate to either. This was the most momentous, if not the most immediately obvious, result of the 1848 revolutions. For,

AFTER THE REVOLUTION

having failed through the actions of its liberals to effect the two conditions most favorable thus far to modernization, Germany now embarked on a different course. With liberals now leading the way, Germans enthusiastically reverted once again to the traditional posture of utilizing the new to reinforce the old. Technology and capitalism, nationalism and pseudoconstitutionalism, progress in higher learning and a nonacademic culture of accommodation and renunciation—all were harnessed to the perpetuation of the old-time autocratic political system and paternal social order.

The failure of the revolutions implied, however, neither the decline of liberalism as a significant force in German affairs after 1850 nor a diminution of interest in its primary goals of *Einheit* and *Freiheit*. On the contrary, if the revolutions accomplished little else, they managed to gain support for the view that Germany's future depended upon unification of some sort with some degree of popular assent, or at least submission, to a central government. To this end, Frederick William IV, king of Prussia from 1840 to 1861, issued a constitution in 1850 that would remain in effect in Prussia until the end of the monarchy in 1918 and serve as a model for Germany's constitution after unification in 1871. It provided for a bicameral Diet, in which the upper house was reserved for the nobility. The lower house was to be elected according to a three-class system of suffrage, based on taxation, whereby about 5 percent of the voters would elect one-third of the deputies, 15 percent another third, and the remaining 80 percent of the population the rest. The army, entirely free from constitutional regulation, would continue to be responsible only to the king. The cabinet ministers also were not to be responsible to the Diet, but only to the king, who had the power to appoint and dismiss them at will. And the principle of divine right was explicitly retained.

Such a constitution was obviously a farce in that it clearly favored the old powerful conservative interests, allocated overwhelming authority to the executive, and rejected representative government as something revolutionary. Even with this constitution, the Prussian monarchy "was still much stronger than the English monarchy [had been] in the seventeenth century, which was already without a standing army behind it. . . . Again, the Prussian lower house, because of three-class suffrage, was even less representative of society than the parliaments of Charles I."[1] Nevertheless, a constitution now existed where none had existed before. This fact alone did much to appease the liberals, which was after all its main purpose. Moreover, the constitution did provide for parliamentary consent to legislation and certain restrictions on the executive. And these scanty powers enabled the liberals to avoid ever becoming merely the docile instruments of what remained an emphatically autocratic system of government.

However, the acceptance of this constitution by the liberals was due mainly to their own outlook and disposition at the time. Even before 1848, the attitude of the German liberal toward the state was more sanguine than that of his Western counterpart. He differed from the Western liberal also in not asserting any absolute claim of the sovereignty of the people or the right of revolution. After 1848, discouraged by defeat, distrustful by tradition of democratization, and fearful of the growing discontent and disenchantment with liberalism of the lower classes, German liberals continued to scale down their aspirations. They were now more inclined than ever to work for their goals piecemeal, to compromise, to seek the "attainable" rather than the "desirable," as the future finance minister of Prussia, Johannes Miquel (1828–1890), put it.

Both before and after 1848, their principal aim was nothing more or less than the transformation of the existing authoritarian state into a *Rechtsstaat*, "by which was meant a constitutional state of civil equality, of subordination of the government to due process of law, of participation by the people in lawmaking and administration, and of individual freedom in spiritual, social, and economic life." [2] The idea of a *Rechtsstaat*—and this was precisely its appeal—rested on the hopeful belief that these goals, which the liberals had failed to achieve by direct political action, could be effected by legal means, even within an unfavorable political environment.[3] Hence, the liberals logically concluded that, under the circumstances, the *Rechtsstaat* could best be realized by means of a constitution, preferably "a mixed constitution with domination by neither the parliament nor the king." [4]

This, of course, was not the constitution they got. Moreover, it is doubtful whether any constitution can be viable, even one less shabby than the Prussian, which is prescribed from above rather than formulated by the representatives of the people. As the constitutional conflict of the 1860's shows, the whole idea of the *Rechtsstaat* was illusory, although it is difficult to see, even in retrospect, what feasible alternative might have been available to German liberals at the time. Still, in an age that honored only *Macht* as the final arbiter of political affairs, the concept of a *Rechtsstaat*, appealing to legality rather than to power, was clearly an anachronism. As for achieving a *Rechtsstaat* by means of a "mixed constitution with domination by neither the parliament nor the king," this was a theory first espoused systematically by a conservative, the eighteenth-century French aristocrat Montesquieu. And his intention, as his own contemporaries recognized, was less to advance the liberal cause than to oppose absolutism in the interest of a feudal revival. However, even Montesquieu claimed that, in case of a stalemate between the executive and legislative branches of government, the legislative should have the upper hand, which was manifestly out of the question in Germany.

Of course, the circumstances of nineteenth-century Germany were not those of eighteenth-century France. Nor was it the aim of German liberals to revive feudalism at the expense of absolutism. But was their liberalism adequate to resist either? This was the critical question. While it would be unhistorical to judge them from the standpoint of twentieth-century liberal democrats, it is also true that Western liberalism was always more susceptible to democratization than the German variety, and that this greater susceptibility was instrumental in saving it from capitulation, at least in the nineteenth century. The tragedy of German liberalism was that capitulation seems to have been built into it from the very start.[5] It was a steady process, beginning long before 1850 and ending well after; a process due to a combination of the impoverishment and timidity of liberal policies and programs, on the one hand, and to the retrograde political and social conditions of Germany on the other.

These issues came to a head during the constitutional conflict of the 1860's, which brought Otto von Bismarck (1815–1898) to the fore in German political life. The immediate question was whether the Diet could effectively veto the new military budget proposed by the government, which would mean additional taxes for the already overtaxed middle classes. Their representatives in the Diet naturally refused to support an army over which they had no control—an army that was contemptuous of the constitution and served the interests of their Junker antagonists. The more fundamental question was what force the constitution would have in such a situation and what role the Diet would actually play in governmental affairs.

In 1862 Bismarck was called upon to cajole the Diet into submission to the king's will. Failing in this, he simply acted in defiance of the constitution and for the next four years continued to collect, illegally, the new taxes, which nobody refused to pay. The sensational victory of Prussia over Austria in 1866 appeased the nationalism of the liberals and enabled Bismarck to persuade parliament to pass a bill of indemnity, which, while acknowledging the government's wrongdoing during the previous four years, retroactively legalized its transactions. When the bill was presented to parliament, the distinguished liberal representative, Karl Twesten (1820–1870), urged its passage, saying: "We cannot blame anyone who, at this time, puts the question of power in the foreground and suggests that questions of freedom can wait, as long as nothing happens which could permanently prejudice our development toward freedom."[6] Bismarck, with his characteristic genius for turning political success abroad to political advantage at home, had suc-

OTTO VON BISMARCK, painting by Franz von Lenbach
Depicts the Iron Chancellor as a stern but concerned leader.

ceeded in building another important bridge between the liberals and the antiliberal government he headed.

Prussia's victory over Austria opened a whole new chapter in German political history. For one thing, it resolved in Prussia's favor the century-long conflict between the two states for hegemony in Germany. In 1867 Prussia easily unified all of Germany north of the Main river into a new political organization known as the North German Confederation. It also split the liberals into two factions: a pro-Bismarck majority, which founded the National Liberal Party in 1867, and an anti-Bismarck minority, the remnants of the old Progressive Party from which the newer one was formed. Bismarck could now proceed with his plans for the unification of all Germany with or without liberal support, although he was to have it henceforward for the most part. Above all, however, German political affairs had been determined once again without either the initiative or consent of the German people. And no force existed any longer capable of resisting that trend.

The final step in German unification came with Prussia's victory over France in 1871. This third and last of Bismarck's wars, the Franco-Prussian war, was intended to serve three interrelated purposes: to force France to accept the existence of a united Germany on her eastern frontier, which her leaders had opposed for three centuries; to sweep the reluctant south German states, of which Bavaria was the largest and most important, into the new political structure; and above all to insure Prussia's predominance within it. The war accomplished all three, and on January 18, 1871, the second German Empire was officially proclaimed at Prussian

PROCLAMATION OF THE GERMAN EMPIRE AT VERSAILLES, JANUARY 1871, painting by Anton von Werner
Captures the note of triumph and the solemnity of the occasion.

headquarters in the palace of Versailles. The new German state was the result of a Prussian military victory over a foreign country in a power struggle abroad. That it was founded on foreign soil at the expense of another sovereign nation, and under the auspices of only one of its constituent members, was a strange and ominous beginning for any new state. Nevertheless, a unified Germany now existed. It was neither *grossdeutsch* (inclusive of Austria) nor precisely *kleindeutsch* (exclusive of Austria) in the older, prerevolutionary sense. Rather, it was *grosspreussisch* (an appendage to Prussia). And it was largely the work of one brilliant politician who sacrificed all else to that end.

What emerged in 1871 was not only a new Germany, but also the most powerful state on the Continent. This was something that no one, including Bismarck himself, could have foreseen only ten years earlier. Such sudden and complete success was sufficient to silence all remaining serious opposition to Bismarck and what he represented: Prussian conservatism, imperial autocracy, and a politics of "blood and iron." Few bothered any longer to raise the question of whether the way in which unification had come about might not, in Karl Twesten's words, have "permanently prejudiced" Germany's development toward freedom. Those who did were now usually, either by choice or necessity, so far removed from the mainstream of German public life that they went almost unnoticed.

But whether Germans at the time recognized it or not, German unification was the product of a course of action that deviated drastically, both in means and motives, from the development of the modern state in the West. Paradoxically, Germany became a state, and assumed a commanding place in the modern world, just when it was less at one in spirit with the West than at any time since the Reformation. One of the most significant aspects of Bismarck's policies during the sixties was precisely to show that similar results could be achieved by different means; that an efficient, up-to-date state could be forged without appeal, and even in opposition, to the theory and practice of statehood in the West. He was, in effect, the first major European diplomatist to demonstrate the possibility of an alternative to modernization other than the Western one.

For Bismarck did not seek unification as a nationalist; nationalism, as a Europeanwide doctrine that aimed at the creation of a popular state, repelled him. And he correctly guessed that unification, in whatever form, would appease the German nationalists anyway. Nor, certainly, did he work for unification to satisfy the liberals, who, as nationalists, aided and applauded him on the assumption that statehood would lead more or less automatically to greater civil freedom. Bismarck's achievement actually disproved that assumption. On the contrary, he utilized unification less as a means to reorganize Germany along modern lines than to preserve it as far as possible in its premodern political and social condition, so as to safeguard and enhance the hegemony of conservative Prussia both within Germany and in the world at large. The result was, according to one recent historian, the unique spectacle of "a great power without a national base."[7] Another aptly calls its founder the century's "greatest conservative revolutionary."[8]

Bismarck devoted the rest of his long and stormy career to the consolidation and protection of his creation. The actions and policies that shaped the new state during the first twenty years of its existence all originated with him: the persecution of the Catholics in the seventies and the socialists in the eighties, the complicated system of alliances with Austria, Russia, and Italy, the social welfare programs, and his role as peacemaker in Europe. His refusal to allow the state that he had created to be transformed or experimented with is what finally led to his dismissal from the office of chancellor in 1890. The legacy he left Germany, however, was an impressive one. It included a viable state, an alliance system to protect it, a federal constitution, and even the beginnings of a colonial empire. But he achieved it by undermining representative institutions and practices, weakening the party system, encouraging social and religious divisiveness, and discouraging the spirit of self-determination.

The German question was finally settled, then, almost single-handedly by a man who understood better than anyone else the politics of the attainable. Princes, aristocrats, and bourgeois; conservatives, liberals, and nationalists; democrats and socialists had little to do with it. Bismarck spoke for none of them, none could prevail upon him to do so, and he skillfully manipulated all of them to his own ends. Even in its hour of triumph, especially then, Germany revealed its incapacity to mobilize the resources, both political and intellectual, foreign and domestic, past and present, that might have enabled society to act on its own behalf. Bismarck succeeded in guiding Germany into the modern age, but his success, which depended so heavily on discrediting these resources and severing Germans from them, did much to intensify the spiritual crisis and loss of identity[9] that carried over from the *Vormärz*.

Such was the political context within which Germany underwent the transition from a predominantly agricultural economy to a streamlined industrial state. Where it took England over a century to complete this transition, Germany experienced it in about thirty years, the last three decades of the nineteenth century. Rapid progress was made after 1850 in the transportation, mining, and chemical industries. This was accompanied and fostered by the growth of banks, stock companies, and credit institutions. The Hamburg–Amerika steamship line was founded in 1847 and the North German Lloyd line in 1857. From small beginnings before 1850, the Krupp ironworks grew into one of the world's mightiest industrial empires by 1900. Along with Krupp, the names of Thyssen, Siemens, and Farben were to become bywords of German heavy industry. Albert Schäffle and the Oppenheimer and Hansemann families figured prominently in the growth of German banking. By the end of the century, Germany had assumed European leadership in large-scale corporate enterprise and mass production. The Germans were also especially prominent in the application of scientific research to technology.

The very rapidity of this process was bound to have a disturbing social effect. In 1871 about 64 percent of the German population still lived in rural areas; by 1910 the figure had dropped to about 40 percent. In Prussia, the population of the agrarian east increased by 91 percent between 1816 and 1871, while the more industrial south and west increased by only 23 percent during the same period. Between 1871 and 1890, however, this trend was reversed. Amid a general upsurge in population, the south and west increased in population by 79 percent and the east by only 26 percent. These figures give some indication of the effects of industrialization on the complexion of German society.

One of the most important of these effects was the quite sudden appearance in large numbers of two new social types, the industrial entrepreneur and the factory worker. Both faced the difficult task of adapting to an inflexible political and social order. Throughout the Bismarckian era, the powerful nobility continued to disdain business and industry. Compared to the French or English aristocrat, the German Junker was far less inclined to intermingle with the upper middle classes. "And only in Germany did the uneducated and impoverished section of the aristocracy, also, still enjoy social importance."[10] The industrialist, for his part, was willing to respect the political privileges and prestige of the Junkers and to accept a subordinate standing in the social order, because he was dependent upon the state for protection against foreign competition and against the working classes at home. It is true that, in the boom period following the Franco-Prussian war, some degree of amalgamation began to take place, especially through intermarriage, which gave to the aristocrat badly needed money and to the middle-class parvenu social prestige. Insofar as a rapprochement did occur, however, it was almost wholly one-sided and served to strengthen rather than weaken the position of the nobility and military circles. Consequently, the business and industrial classes, although they enjoyed great prosperity and controlled a vast portion of the country's wealth, remained almost completely without political power right up to the First World War.[11] By the same token, their acquiescence aided Bismarck in consolidating a power base for his state, founded on the uneasy reconciliation of these two historically antagonistic social elements.[12]

The new industrialist and entrepreneur also supported the Bismarckian state because industrialization came too late in Germany to be very vitally influenced by the ideas and ideals which had infused it in the West.[13] The growth of science and technology in France had been linked with the rationalist Enlightenment and the Revolution; and, in England, with the philosophy of utilitarianism and individualism. In Germany, they grew up in an ethos characterized by disillusionment with these values. Pessimism, positivism, and materialism prevailed in German thought in the late nineteenth century; and nationalism, imperialism, and the worship of power in political life. The expansive economic drive of the German middle classes paralleled, and found inspiration in, the expansive political drive of Bismarck's Prussia. They thoroughly relished Germany's newly won glory and were proud to be a part of it. Even their attitudes and conduct often aped those of the ruling classes, as in their strict devotion to duty, the iron discipline with which they ruled over their families, and their view of the business enterprise as a sort of personal dynasty to be bequeathed eventually to children taught to follow in their fathers' footsteps. However, a subtle effect of this complicated relationship between Junker and bourgeois—an effect brilliantly treated in the novels of Theodor Fontane and in other writings of the period—was not to strengthen but to shake the self-confidence of both, since each was well aware that the other's existence threatened his own.

The new urban proletariat was even less easily assimilable to the existing social order than its employers. Regarded by supporters of the Bismarck regime as *Reichsfeinde* (enemies of the state), and distrustful of and distrusted by the middle-class liberals who willingly cooperated with the regime, workers turned to the German Workers' Party, founded in 1863 by the brilliant young socialist Ferdinand Lassalle (1825–1864). A follower of Marx, Lassalle made his teacher's radical views the basis of the new party's program. On certain key points, however, he departed from Marx: in his advocacy of universal suffrage instead of revolution as the best means to achieve socialist goals, in his acceptance of the legitimacy of the state as already constituted, and in his emphasis on the national rather than on the international growth of socialism. These modifications were embodied in the Gotha program (1875), which became for a time the official program of the new party that now called itself the Social Democratic Party. Lassalle's innovations actually drew the teeth of Marxism, but they also enabled the party to survive and thrive in the autocratic regime, and to become by

1912 the largest and most important single party in Germany. Lassalle and Bismarck even developed a liking for one another, based on these concessions and on their mutual detestation of the middle classes.

The party grew so rapidly during the seventies that, in 1878, Bismarck enacted a series of antisocialist laws, which remained in effect until 1890. They allowed the government to suppress all independent labor organizations and all socialist publications, associations, and meetings. When the laws were lifted, the party, now under the leadership of August Bebel (1840–1913), adopted a more strictly Marxist position, as embodied in the so-called Erfurt program, which was drawn up in 1891 under the guidance of the new socialist luminary Karl Kautsky (1845–1938). With this program the German socialists soon assumed leadership of the European socialist movement as a whole, notwithstanding the emergence within their ranks of a "revisionist" faction, headed by Eduard Bernstein (1850–1932) who hearkened back to Lassalle's views.

In spite of its size and influence, however, the German Social Democratic party had curiously little effect on practical politics, and a deep gulf continued to separate it from the rest of German society until the First World War. Although the orthodox socialists consistently expressed their adamant opposition to the bourgeoisie, voting in the Reichstag against military expenditures and colonial expansion, they often shared their opponents' shortcomings. Their leaders, Lassalle and Bebel in particular, were often doctrinaire and autocratic in their approach to the party, treating it frequently as a sort of personal dynasty. The membership was taught to pride itself on its insularity and aloofness from the rest of society. Bold theories were not backed up by effective action, and loudly proclaimed principles and goals were often sacrificed to expediency and immediate gain. By the turn of the century, the party was already less threatening than it appeared to be. In a quarrel with Bebel at the Socialist International in 1904, the French socialist leader, Jean Jaurés (1859–1914), accurately hit upon the chief defect of the German socialists:[14]

You still lack the two essential parts, the two essential means for action by the proletariat: you have neither revolutionary action nor parliamentary action. . . . You mask your powerlessness of action before your own proletariat and before the international proletariat by seeking refuge in the intransigence of theoretical formulas . . . .

The socialists, like the liberals, found themselves in a deeply ambivalent position. And on August 4, 1914, the Social Democratic deputies to the Reichstag voted along with the others in favor of the war credits sought by the government.

Along with these political and social developments, higher education also underwent important changes during the Bismarckian era.[15] The German university gradually ceased to be considered, as it traditionally had been, a bastion of moral truth and cultural excellence. Nor was it to be any longer a haven from the world at large, where students and scholars might devote themselves to self-perfection, such as Wilhelm von Humboldt and other educational reformers of the early part of the century had conceived it. Instead, the university began now to concentrate on practical affairs and preparation for participating in them. Philosophy and philology, traditional strongholds of German learning, began to give way to the empirical sciences and speculation to factual research. Idealism, as the guiding spirit of scholarship, was supplanted by positivism and synthesis by specialization. Interest shifted from theological and metaphysical disputes to historical and political issues. And the prime purpose of the university was no longer to provide a humanistic education, but rather to be a training ground for bureaucrats, technicians, and specialists in all fields.

Students no longer came only from the ranks of the aristocracy and upper middle classes; they now came from lower middle-class, working-class, and even peasant backgrounds. A university degree became now both an economic and a social advantage. And university graduates were no longer content to be private tutors, pastors, and minor administrators. With their greater expertise, professionalism, and industriousness, they could now command, in their accelerating society, more respectable and rewarding work. Thus, the traditional separation of the university from society began to disappear. In the process, however, the independent, the critical, and the dissenting voices also began to disappear from the university.

Not surprisingly, then, the Bismarckian power-state found a great source of support in the universities. Each served the other. Ever since the days of the *Burschenschaften,* the university had been a focus of political ferment and the dream of national unification. Once that dream became reality, the educated saw little reason not to welcome it enthusiastically. The expanding new state gave them new pride in being German and opened up new and greater outlets for their talents. More people from a broader range of social backgrounds could make use of higher education to serve themselves and society. And the revision of educational objectives gave them a new sense of relevance to the contemporary world.

Some of the strongest intellectual support for the second Reich came from historians,[16] especially the so-called Prussian school, headed by Johann Gustav Droysen (1808–1884), Heinrich von Sybel (1817–1895), and Heinrich von Treitschke (1834–1896). They followed the lead of Leopold von Ranke (1795–1886), the doyen of nineteenth-century German historians, who viewed history primarily in political terms, in contrast to the broader, more philosophical approach of the earlier Hegelians and romantics. Ranke was a strict empiricist, who urged historians not to judge the past, but only to describe it accurately, by means of careful, first-hand research into the original sources. He was also a relativist, who held that all ages and peoples are equal in the sight of God, and that the historian should, therefore, be impartial in his treatment of them. His prestige as a professor and the success of his historical masterpieces gained prominence for his views in academic circles, through which they were then imparted to educated Germans and to large numbers of foreigners who studied in Germany in the late nineteenth century.

Ranke's theory of the equality of all ages and peoples before God was in fact tacitly prejudicial to the idea of historical progress. In reality, however, he dealt almost exclusively in his writings with the Latin and Germanic peoples, implying thereby that they actually occupied a special place in the sight of God. In contrast to the earlier historical conceptions of Herder, Hegel, and the romantics, Ranke's Europe-centered vision left little room for speculation about the role of Russia, America, and other non-European areas in the course of world history. Moreover, by restricting the historian's task so exclusively to a factual description of the past, to a recounting of things as they actually were and not as they might have been or might be, he left little room for a consideration of the possible and undocumentable, which are also important to a proper understanding of history. And, by concentrating on the political past, he left little room for an evaluation of the hitherto politically neglected, the inactive, the anonymous, and the unsuccessful, as well as of nonpolitical factors in the life of society. Finally, Ranke's recommendation to historians to refrain from the moral and critical judgment of an age or people was bound to favor a spirit of accommodation to the existing order of things. In these respects, too, Ranke's teachings proved influential.

For it was only a short step from asserting the absoluteness of the factual to asserting the factuality of the absolute; that is, to generalizing the factual into the inevitable and the inevitable into the just. Thus, in spite of Ranke's appeal for objectivity and impartiality on the part of historians, the active support of the second *Reich* by the Prussian historians was not really logically inconsistent with his views. Nor was history, conceived as political history, really so far removed from the utilization of history as a means of politicization. The centrality of Europe, and only Western Europe at that, to Ranke's conception of universal history could easily lead to an exaggeration of the importance of specifically German affairs. And his contrary claim, that the whole of the past was of equal value from the standpoint of God, conveniently disposed of the question of whether, and to what extent, the new Germany served or impeded progress from the human standpoint.

This was Ranke's legacy to the Prussian school of historians who, as the name suggests, undertook to reinterpret German history, so as to show Prussia's role in it in the most favorable light. Far more than any other school of German historians, they involved themselves in public life, and, through their professorships and writings, actively sought to shape public opinion. Treitschke, a great publicist as well as a great historian, turned out to be the chief intellectual advocate of the Bismarckian state. He used his talents to great effect, after 1871, to propagate the antiliberal, antidemocratic, antisocialist, anti-Catholic, anti-Semitic, imperalist policies implemented by the new regime. Before Prussia's defeat of Austria, all of these historians had subscribed to the ideals of 1848, and, during the constitutional conflict of the sixties, tended to be critical of Bismarck's autocratic views and high-handed methods. After 1866, their resistance turned into support. This abrupt about-face was possible because, as disillusioned liberals, they were already prepared, if necessary, to sacrifice *Freiheit* to *Einheit;* and, as historians with positivist leanings, they were already prepared to equate fact with value. There was no arguing with success. Thereafter, especially for Treitschke, it was a matter of rapid capitulation to most of what the second *Reich* stood for. Droysen spoke for them all, when he asserted: "In the world of politics the law of force has the same validity as the law of gravity in the physical world." [17]

Thus, the educated classes, along with the others, were swept on the crest of success into acceptance of the new power-state. The critical, the dissenting, and the most creative minds of the time were no longer to be found in the universities as a rule, nor even in the mainstream of German life in general. They were no longer respected, or at least tolerated, as they had been in Goethe's time. Nor were they still close enough to public affairs to be considered as dangerous nuisances, as they were during the *Vormärz.* They were now so isolated, physically and spiritually, as to be, with a few notable exceptions, unknown or ignored. They formed no schools or movements and attracted no followings. They existed, both sociologically and geographically, on the margin of the new society: in the countryside; in small towns, passed over by industrialization; or else abroad. Their discontent with Bismarckian Germany assumed a variety of interrelated forms. Three of them, to be dealt with in the following section, might be classified as a quest for rejuvenation, renunciation, and denunciation.

Notes to Chapter Seven

1. Walter M. Simon, *Germany: A Brief History* (New York: Random House, 1966), p. 200.
2. Gordon R. Mork, "Political Ferment in Bismarckian Germany: The National Liberals." Paper delivered at the annual meeting of the Pacific Coast Branch of the American Historical Association (August 30, 1968), p. 2.
3. See Rupert Emerson, *State and Sovereignty in Modern Germany* (New Haven: Yale University Press, 1928), Chapters 2 and 3. See also Leonard Krieger, *The German Idea of Freedom* (Boston: Beacon Press, 1957), Chapters 7 and 8.
4. Mork, *op. cit.,* p. 3.
5. See Friedrich C. Sell, *Die Tragödie des Deutschen Liberalismus* (Stuttgart: Deutsche-Verlags Anstalt, 1953).
6. Quoted in Mork, *op. cit.,* p. 4.
7. Helmuth Plessner, *Die Verspätete Nation* (Stuttgart: Kohlhammer, 1959), p. 42.
8. Wilhelm Schüssler, *Um das Geschichtsbild* (Freizeiten: Gladbeck, 1953), p. 129.
9. A good case in point is the following criticism of the conservatives by the socialist, Wilhelm Liebknecht (1826–1900): "Now gentlemen, in 1866, you took your stand for the policy of annexations, that is, for the revolution from above. In doing so, the conservative carpet was irretrievably pulled from beneath your feet. From that moment onward, when you declared yourselves in favor of the revolutionary principles of annexation, for universal suffrage, for popular sovereignty, you ceased to be a Conservative Party." Quoted in Robert M. Berdahl, "Political Ferment in Bismarckian Germany: The Prussian Conservatives." Paper delivered at the annual meeting of the Pacific Coast Branch of the American Historical Association (August 30, 1968), p. 3.

   Much the same could be said of the other political parties and factions during the 1880's: liberals had ceased to be liberal, democrats to be democratic, socialists to be socialistic, and so on.
10. Ernest K. Bramsted, *Aristocracy and the Middle Classes in Germany: Social Types in German Literature, 1830–1900,* rev. ed. (Chicago: Phoenix Books, 1964), p. 229.
11. See Koppel S. Pinson, *Modern Germany,* 2nd ed. (New York: Macmillan, 1966), pp. 250–251.
12. See Arthur Rosenberg, *Imperial Germany: The Birth of the German Republic, 1871–1918,* trans. by I. F. D. Morrow, 2nd ed. (Boston: Beacon Press, 1964), Chapters 1 and 2.
13. See William J. Bossenbrook, *The German Mind* (Detroit: Wayne State University, 1961), pp. 337 ff.
14. Quoted in Pinson, *op. cit.,* pp. 217–218.
15. See Frederic Lilge, *The Abuse of Learning: The Failure of the German University* (New York: Macmillan, 1948).
16. See Georg G. Iggers, *The German Conception of History* (Middletown, Conn.: Wesleyan University Press, 1968), Chapters 4 and 5. See also Gerhard Schilfert, "Leopold von Ranke," and Hans Schleier, "Die kleindeutsche Schule," both in *Studien über die Deutsche Geschichtswissenschaft,* ed. by Joachim Streisand (Berlin: Akademie-Verlag, 1969), Vol. I, pp. 241 ff.
17. Quoted in Iggers, *ibid.,* p. 114.

Can it be the true vocation of the German people to form a great centralized state when their entire history speaks out to the contrary? Can it be their vocation to break with their long historic past, to set up in its place an order dictated solely by utilitarian considerations?

Konstantin Frantz

The second *Reich*, based as it was on a precarious amalgamation of new and old, did not fully satisfy any faction of German society. At the same time, since it represented such a drastic and rapid departure from what had gone before, all factions experienced some degree of social and spiritual dislocation. The new Germany was neither the conservative ideal of a *Ständesstaat* nor the liberal ideal of a *Rechsstaat*. It lacked the supranational character of a true empire, but it also lacked the popular base of a modern, secular nation-state. Despite the overwhelming acceptance of the Prussian solution to the German problem, therefore, voices of protest began to be heard.

Frantz, Lagarde, Wagner: Mission and Myth

One of the most important was that of Konstantin Frantz (1817–1891), a conservative opponent of Bismarck's Prussia-centered Germany and the leading spokesman in his time for a federated Central Europe under German leadership.[1] This theory he expounded in a series of pamphlets, written between 1870 and 1890, wherein he claimed that the Bismarckian state represented an aberration from Germany's true political and spiritual traditions, as embodied in the medieval Holy Roman Empire. Instead, he claimed that the new state presented an obstacle to Germany's organic development toward a revived pan-German Christian empire, which would be consistent with those earlier traditions. According to Frantz, Bismarck had simply absorbed Germany into

THE CULTURE OF REJECTION

8

a godless, materialistic Prussia, had debased the German spirit by the example of his own vulgar pursuit of power, and had set the new state on a collision course with the British empire. What the world situation called for was a Germany strong enough within Europe to offset the global might of Britain and France, Russia and America. Only a federation of all the peoples of Central Europe, and not simply their annexation by Prussia, could provide such a counterpoise. What the internal German situation called for was a spiritual regeneration along universal Christian lines, in order to counteract the ill effects of Germany's departure from her political past under Bismarck and to justify a position of leadership for Germany in a multinational, ethnically and culturally mixed federation. Probably Frantz's most valuable insight was precisely that, if Germany were to survive and thrive within the modern state system, it would need a *raison d'être* in the form of a far broader foundation and appeal than that provided by Bismarck's narrowly based *Machtstaat.*

In some respects, Frantz's federalism was but a revised version of the earlier *grossdeutsch* theory, which advocated the political unification of all German-speaking people, including the Austrians and others settled in East Central Europe. But whereas this theory had been supported mainly by liberals in the 1840's, Frantz, writing in the aftermath of its defeat, sought to revive it from an ultra-conservative and frankly mystical standpoint. The liberals had advocated the *grossdeutsch* form of unification on the grounds that it would be more inclusive of the German people as a whole and would, therefore, more truly resemble a modern nation-state. Frantz approved it for exactly the opposite reason; namely, that it was the only available theory consistent with Germany's premodern political and spiritual traditions. His objection to the second *Reich* was that it was too modern, too westernized, and hence too un-German. For Frantz, although he repudiated Bismarck's *Realpolitik,* was strongly opposed also to constitutional government, representative institutions, and democracy; to nationalism, capitalism, and the emancipation of the Jews; and to any form of secular progress whatever. He favored the *grossdeutsch* solution precisely because he thought it would guarantee Germany's future by restoring its Christian imperial past. Innovation he opposed in the name of rejuvenation.

Frantz's views were not widely publicized in his time; his idea of a federated Central Europe came into its own only much later, after World War Two. But he already foreshadowed the pan-German and neoromantic youth movements that would emerge in force in the 1890's. Moreover, his teachings illustrated[2] *the curious fact that it was precisely those elements opposed to militaristic Prussia who elaborated an ideology of Central European expansionism, which in this respect went far beyond the nationalism of the* kleindeutsch *followers. The subsequent pan-German movement is probably much more the heir of the anti-Prussian than of the pro-Prussian tradition in German history.*

Another protester in the name of rejuvenation was Paul de Lagarde (1827–1891).[3] Like Frantz, Lagarde was a severe critic of Bismarck, an adamant opponent of modernism in all of its manifestations, and a conservative advocate of the *grossdeutsch* theory as the best political means by which to reconstruct Germany's former imperial greatness. Also like Frantz, Lagarde believed that Germany could resist the evils of modern society and recover its true identity only by means of a religious rebirth. As a Biblical scholar, Lagarde had concluded early in his career that the original spirit of Christianity, as embodied in the life of Jesus and in the gospel, had been betrayed by all subsequent religious developments. Judaism, Catholicism, and even Protestantism were all to blame. The corruption of religion, he held, had corrupted the spirit, and that in turn had paved the way for the appearance of all the evils that plague modern society. What Lagarde proposed, therefore, was a spiritual rebirth in the form of a new religion that would be appropriate to and serve the national character. It would be a distinctively Germanic Christian faith, originating among the common people rather than in the educated classes, who had been led astray by foreign and wrong-headed theological doctrines.

Up to a point, Lagarde's plans for the spiritual reform of Germany hearkened back to the older, romantic conception of a dichotomy between the (good) *Volk* and the (evil) state. However, the earlier romantics had not conceived the *Volk* as being always and necessarily antimodern; nor had all of them equated virtue with opposition to the present, as Lagarde did. On the contrary, Schlegel, Hölderlin, Heine, and others had often praised the *Volk* and the folk-hero for defying tradition, for opposing the backward conditions of German society, and for championing progress. Unlike Lagarde, they delighted in the experimental, the sensual, the unpopular, and the underdog.

Lagarde, on the other hand, viewed the *Volk* as but passive victims of modernization and the state as but the instrument of its victimization. Accordingly, he praised the *Volk* as a bulwark to progress, which he denounced as a foreign force. To a greater extent than the romantics, even the most reactionary of them, Lagarde equated moral good with the Germanic and evil with the foreign. Thus, the cosmopolitanism characteristic of the earlier romantics

Lagarde abandoned in favor of extreme chauvinism, which set Germanism above and against everything and everyone else. The lively interest of the early romantics in the concrete folkways, traditions, and ethos of German folk culture; their delight in its variety, earthiness, and humor Lagarde transmuted into a hazy, mystical conception of a universal, spiritual *Volk* mission, similar to that espoused at about the same time by the Slavophiles in Russia. Whereas the romantics had typically held that German folk culture was good because it was human, Lagarde believed that it was good because it was German. At bottom, Lagarde's peculiar adaptation of romantic attitudes stemmed from the fact that "his ambitions were not born of the conviction of Germany's greatness; they arose instead from the misgivings about Germany's fate which so oppressed his mind."[4]

The most impressive advocate of rejuvenation by far was Richard Wagner (1813–1883),[5] whose artistic genius and influence on late nineteenth-century European culture were unsurpassed. Like Frantz, Lagarde, and other conservative visionaries, Wagner fulminated against the *embourgeoisement* of life and culture in imperial Germany in the name of a supposedly ideal Germanic past. Unlike them, however, he searched for the sources of Germany's regeneration not in history and politics, but in art and myth. As a continuator of romanticism, Wagner realized that an artist, when he deliberately frees himself from reality's limitations, can usually produce a bolder, more powerful vision of things than if he addresses himself directly to reality. He recognized also that art and myth have a greater emotional appeal and psychological impact than other forms of expression and can serve better to express and evoke supposedly timeless, archetypal, primeval thoughts and feelings. Wagner, who thought of himself as much a prophet and savior as an artist, had both the ambition and talent to mobilize these means for the creation, or re-creation, of an ancient, heroic, purely Germanic view of existence.

Wagner, of course, was not the first to make use of myth as an artistic means to serve society. The classicists had utilized Greek myth and the romantics medieval legend to similar ends. In their hands, however, myth served to uphold what they believed were the normative values of civilization; to represent, symbolically, the best that had actually been realized at various times throughout the ages. Even Novalis, whose view of life and conception of art resembled Wagner's in many ways, thought of himself in the final analysis as a poetic spokesman for Christian values.

Wagner, by contrast, who was deeply influenced by Schopenhauer and his pessimistic view of life, regarded myth as the antithesis of civilization. He thought of myth as the primeval, supposedly "purely human"[6] source from which all civilization had sprung, but which civilization in turn had destroyed in the course of time. The myths which inspired Wagner were neither Greek nor Christian, but rather the primitive, pre-Christian sagas of the ancient Nordic *Edda,* which he set over against civilized and Christian values. True, some of his heroes bear a resemblance to Christian figures and motifs, as Siegfried does to Christ. In fact, however, Siegfried, and later Parsifal, are strictly Germanic heroes, who supplant Christ as savior figures in Wagner's art, as art replaces religion altogether as the means to redeem mankind. Wagner stated in his famous essay *Art and Religion* (1880):[7]

One could say that when religion becomes artificial, it remains for art to salvage its true essence by perceiving its mythical symbols—which religion would have us believe as the literal truth—only according to their figurative value, in order to make us see their profound, hidden truth through idealized representation.

But a contemporary critic notes that "*Parsifal* is an independent Wagnerian religion, a religion of art, essentially alien to Christianity even though the opera seems to suggest a Christian milieu with some Buddhism thrown in for good measure."[8]

Wagner masterfully developed this vision of the world in one massive, monumental opera after another—*The Flying Dutchman* (1841), *Tannhäuser* (1845), *Lohengrin* (1848), *The Ring of the Nibelungen* (1852), *Tristan and Isolde* (1865), *The Meistersinger* (1868), *The Götterdämmerung* (1874), *Parsifal* (1882), and others. In each of these theatrical extravaganzas, Wagner explored some aspect of the confrontation between his mythical Germanic warrior- and poet-heroes and an unredeemed, unredeemable society. Neither traditional religion, nor politics, nor erotic love is capable of saving mankind from its morally corrupt state. Only the deceptiveness of art and art conceived as willful deception can reconcile the hero with the world, because it allows him knowingly to perceive and re-create the world through his imagination. The imagination renders the meaninglessness of existence bearable, by transforming the world of reality into symbol and symbol into reality. The two are mutually exclusive; the one presupposes the negation of the other. The rare individual who succeeds in reconciling them, like Hans Sachs in *The Meistersinger,* or Parsifal, are entitled to serve by example as leaders of the rest of mankind. Such was the essence of Wagner's religion of art—a fantastic, elitist, Germanic cult.

The greatness and enormous appeal of Wagner's art lay in his incomparable ability to activate the mythopoeic faculty of the human mind, to present it as something not dead and past, but as a vital, contemporaneous, unifying element of our mental makeup. In this, he anticipated Nietzsche, Freud, the symbolists, and a host of others throughout Europe who concerned themselves with the subconscious, irrational, and symbolic aspects of human behavior. Wagner enhanced his views by appeal to the older, romantic ideal of a "total" work of art. This technique sought, with the help of a leitmotif, to fuse all of the arts—music, poetry, drama, dance, and scenery—into a single unified work designed to stimulate all the senses and emotions, the intellect and imagination simultaneously. Through Wagner's influence, this technique was adopted by Richard Strauss, Gustav Mahler, Anton Bruckner, and others. At Wagner's own theater in Bayreuth, built for him by his adoring, weak-willed patron, King Ludwig II of Bavaria, the audiences were seated without regard to distinctions in rank or importance. This was done to emphasize the theater's role as a place for social regeneration as well as for entertainment. Thus, despite his esoteric themes and dark pessimism, his offensive personal manner and coarse chauvinism, his ill-conceived Germanophilism and virulent anti-Semitism, Wagner achieved a degree of success and popularity that extended far beyond Germany and beyond that of all the other less talented and more conventional exponents of rejuvenation.

The advocates of rejuvenation were, on the one hand, dreamers and "utopians in reverse,"[9] whose hazy yearnings for an idealized past, characterized by spiritual harmony and social solidarity, did more to articulate and stimulate latent discontent with the Bismarckian regime than to change it. Their call for a new state (Frantz), a new religion (Lagarde), and a new culture (Wagner) were just so many ineffectual protests against the secularization and modernization of Germany, which were, for the time being at least, easily ignored or accommodated. Their appeals to emotion and faith, tradition and myth, nationalism and hero worship, rather than to reason, consensus, power, and action, did little to endanger the new state. On the contrary, these appeals could be utilized, when need arose, to gain support for the state, since they lent themselves to a wide variety of interpretations and applications. The dilemma of the rejuvenators was that they could neither abide the new society, nor offer a feasible alternative to it.

However, these outsiders based their unrealizable ideals on one valuable insight, which allowed them to play, successfully, the role of alter ego. More than anyone else, supporters of the new order and critics alike, they grasped the revolutionary implications of Bismarck's work. Their accusation that the new Germany was incompatible with the old was essentially correct. Their analysis of the overall instability of the new Germany was essentially correct. Their claim of the breakdown of traditional cultural values was also sound, as was their sense of the crisis of consciousness engendered by this breakdown. The sudden surge of intellectual movements, like neoromanticism (of which they were a part), neo-

Kantianism, and neo-Hegelianism; the emergence of pan-Germanism in the 1880's and of the primitivist youth movements in the 1890's; and the sharp upsurge of anti-Semitism were all symptomatic of this impending crisis. In addition, the rejuvenators recognized, more or less instinctively, that, where there is a drastic breakdown in continuity and loss of the past, myth can serve better than any other means to suggest the idea of rebirth, return, and reconciliation. It provides a new sense of identity, which operates by excluding those with different origins, traditions, and customs.

Men like Frantz, Lagarde, and Wagner were in a unique position to reveal these insights. For they were not, and did not seek to be, conservatives in the usual sense, since what they wished to conserve no longer existed. Nor were they, strictly speaking, reactionaries, since they did not wish literally to restore the past and substitute it for the present. Instead, their intent was to establish an inviolable continuity between past, present, and future, taking a fictionalized version of the past as normative. They were, in a sense, cultural counterrevolutionaries; or, as one recent commentator labels them, "disinherited conservatives, who had nothing to conserve, because the spiritual values of the past had largely been buried and the material remnants of conservative power did not interest them. They sought a breakthrough to the past, and they longed for a new community in which old ideas and institutions would once again command universal allegiance." [10]

THE ISLE OF THE DEAD, Arnold Böcklin
A visual expression of the mystical, mythological mood of Wagner and the German culture of rejection as it took shape in the late nineteenth century.

(Courtesy, The Metropolitan Museum of Art, Reisinger Fund, 1926)

Renunciation in German Literature

Are they love-words, confided to the wind
And on the way blown away?
Or is it sadness from days to come
That busily strives to make itself heard?
                                    Theodor Storm

The most notable change that came over German literature after 1850 was its disassociation from the mainstream of German life.[11] No German writer of the second half of the century achieved the stature or international reputation of a Dickens or Thackeray, a Flaubert or Zola, a Tolstoy or Dostoevsky. Nor did any equal the accomplishments of their former countrymen, Goethe and Schiller, Kleist, Hölderlin, and Büchner. At the very moment when the novel was reaching its zenith elsewhere in Europe, and the literati were turning their attention to the great social and political issues of the day, the German writer was disengaging himself from the world of affairs, retreating to very limited surroundings, turning inward, and seeking literary forms other than the novel appropriate to this trend. He found it too difficult to reconcile involvement in the realities of late nineteenth-century German society with what he conceived to be his artistic and human integrity. This tendency did not signify that the German writer was less talented or ambitious than his English, French, or Russian counterpart. It did mean that he was more thoroughly estranged from the large world of affairs than they; that he was less able to find in it suitable or inspiring material for great literary works, or a reading public for whom he could write and with whom he could identify; and that his social background, his perspectives on society, and his human ideals were not equal to coping with it as well artistically.

Even the best of German literature after 1850 was provincial by comparison. The better writers lived, in every respect, on the fringe of society. Gottfried Keller (1819–1890) and Conrad Ferdinand Meyer (1825–1898) were Swiss; Adalbert Stifter (1805–1868) was Austrian; Wilhelm Raabe (1831–1910) spent most of his life in a succession of provincial capitals; Theodor Storm (1817–1888) rarely left his beloved Schleswig town of Husum; and Theodor Fontane (1818–1898), the writer most concerned with his social milieu, concentrated on the Brandenburg Mark, the land and people he knew and loved so well. Most of these writers were most productive between 1870 and 1890; yet none of them dealt with the major developments taking place in Germany during those decades: unification, industrialization, urbanization, and the emergence of Germany as a great world power. Nor did they deal much with the new business and industrial classes. They concerned themselves rather with the old nobility, the old patrician classes, the petty bourgeoisie, and the rural classes; those classes in which most of them had their roots and the very ones being left farthest behind in Germany's march toward modernization. It is not surprising, therefore, that they were even more indifferent to space, time, and historical perspective than their predecessors.

German literature during this period is sad, somber, and austere in tone, with undertones of irony and dark humor, which served as a refuge from a threatening world. Schopenhauerian pessimism and disconsolation pervade it, and the motifs of fate, necessity, and defeat are frequently encountered. Strains of classicism, romanticism, and idealism carry over, but they are found wanting, inadequate as guides to the artistic comprehension and mastery of the new realities. Neither history, nature, nor the idea of an immanent rationale in the course of events inspired the writers of the Bismarckian era. Where they do come into play, as in the historical tragedies of Friedrich Hebbel (1813–1863), and in some of the prose and poetry of Keller, Stifter, and Storm, they serve more as sources of consolation and alternatives to human reality than as essential components of it. All in all, many German writers found themselves deprived of most of their inherited social and spiritual functions, a crucial aspect of their existence humorously satirized in the following verse by Theodor Fontane:[12]

"And what's your calling?"
"Writer, Your Majesty. I scribble verses."
The king could not forbear to smile. "Indeed,
I do believe you, sir! For only fools
Would boast of such a trade, or even speak of it
Unless they were obliged to. Ridicule
Will be your portion, not much else, I fear,
Poète allemand!"

Within these limits, however, German literature after 1850 represents an impressive and unique achievement. Precisely because the German writer of this period typically did lack or ignore historical perspective, he was able to discover beauty, humanity, and universality in out-of-the-way places and among declining social types and simple people. Theodor Storm could make the stern German North Sea coast and the modest life of its forgotten inhabitants seem the most important things on earth—largely because he believed it himself. And Stifter's many captivating accounts of a partly real, partly imaginary Austrian countryside and its simple people make the rest of the world seem very far away and unimportant. In all of this the German writer found himself evolving a sort of counterculture, a counterculture of places and people being left behind by history.

Since German writers of this period chose not to contend with history-in-the-making, they could devote themselves more fully to the exploration of universal human themes. Their writings still echo with the great human ideals of an earlier age, which had all but disappeared from other areas of German cultural life. And, by disengaging these themes from the clutter of events, circumstances, and particulars surrounding them, the writer could make use of literary forms more concentrated than the novel; the short story, the poem, the drama, and especially the *Novelle,* in which the German writer of this period excelled. Most important, he found himself, consciously or not, seeking a solution to the perennial problem of the German writer: what to do when all vital contact between the artist and society has broken down. The writer of the Bismarckian era did not put his art in the service of a call to action, nor was he primarily interested in instructing, distracting, or amusing his readers. His solution was a thoroughgoing renunciation of society at large in the name of ideal human values and relationships to be found only in its backwash, in ways of life in the final throes of disintegration. All of this was telling testimony of a failing society and its inability to breach the gap between past and present in a humanly satisfactory way. It testified also to the victimization of the artist and his abdication from striving to influence the course of events.

Theodor Storm and *The Rider on the White Horse*

Storm, in many respects, typified the posture of the German writer of this period. Almost all of the life and writings of this gifted lyric poet and master of the *Novelle* revolved around his birthplace, the tiny Frisian seaport town of Husum. Within this provincial setting, however, he was able to give powerful poetic utterance to the great universal themes of death, unhappy love, inarticulate inwardness, the pain of departures, and the beauty and force of nature, especially the sea. This quality in his work was appreciated by such diverse writers as Gottfried Keller, Theodor Fontane, and Ivan Turgenev. Few other writers (Thomas Wolfe was one) have been able to harmonize local color and the timelessly human so well as Storm. Basic to both writers also was the recurrent longing for home. "If I could just get back again!" Storm laments in a moving poem.[13] "That is perfect Husumania," Thomas Mann called it. "It has almost nothing to do with the soil; it is 'temperament' in the purest cult, the utmost sublimation; nostalgia as idea, home as 'mystery.'"[14] Indeed, for Wolfe as well as for Storm, "the main thing is not to get on in the world but to get home."[15]

Home, for Storm, however, was not a safe and stable or a secure and comfortable place; it was more like a reed in a tempest.

Hence, his nostalgia for it, his need to sublimate and surround it with mystery, even as he lived in its very midst. As an artist, Storm could create and convey this conception brilliantly. But, at the same time, he showed little understanding of how or why the people and way of life he loved so well were coming to an end. Consequently, he could neither judge of the defects of life at home and the vitality of life beyond, nor evolve a meaningful interpretation, whether explicit or implied, of the overall course of things. "Storm could not summon to his aid any substantial and sustaining view of history; of the way in which things had come about or of how they were moving he had little perception." [16] Other German writers of the time, like Gustav Freytag, Wilhelm Raabe, and Theodor Fontane, who shared many of his sympathies and attitudes, often showed a better understanding and appreciation of the forces undermining their provincial domains, even if they did not admire those forces. This difference becomes apparent by comparing Storm's "If I could just get back again!" to a statement by the character, Asche, in Raabe's *Pfister's Mill* (1884):[17]

And you, my lad, don't you imagine that I have come out to Pfister's mill in order to distil end-of-the-world feelings from this stunk-out idyll of your father's pub. Idylls are all very well; but in spite of a melancholy tear for Christmas, Easter, and Whitsun, I now intend to go quietly down among the philistines and there, on that given, bitterly real soil, I intend to guzzle and swig with the rest, to prosper, and if possible to propagate too.

Since Storm did not seek to relate his subject matter to history and society in the large, he avoided the full-length novel in favor of the more economical form of the *Novelle,* of which he became in his time the foremost adept and champion. Against Goethe's older conception of the *Novelle,* Storm wrote: "The *Novelle* is no longer what it once was, 'the succinct presentation of an event, which attracts by its unusual nature and reveals an unexpected turning-point.'"[18] In other words, a literary form that Goethe would have considered appropriate for dealing only with the unusual or atypical, as judged from the comprehensive vantage point of nature or history, seemed to Storm to have a greater potential. For him, the advantage of the *Novelle*—and the reason why it lent itself so well to his purpose and perspective—was precisely that it allowed the author to isolate a fragment of reality, no matter what its status in relation to the whole, and to invest that fragment with all the significance and seriousness worthy of the whole itself or any other of its components. Storm's approach did indeed reveal both the potentialities and the limitations of the *Novelle.* The *Novelle* gives the unusual its due, but at the price of not recognizing or stating that it is unusual. Starting from the premise that Goethe's definition was wrong, Storm went on to give his own view, which no other writer of his day lived up to better than he:[19]

The Novelle *of today is the sister of the drama and the severest form of prose fiction. Like the drama it treats of the profoundest problems of human life; like the drama it demands for the perfections of its form a central conflict from which the whole is organized and in consequence the most succinct form and the exclusion of all that is unessential. It not only accepts but actually makes the biggest demands of art.*

Storm came closest to fulfilling his ideal of the *Novelle* in *The Rider on the White Horse* (1886–1888), his last and greatest story, and one of the best prose works of the time.[20] Of all his writings, it is also the one that comes closest to relating the particular subject matter to a broader context. The story is a reworking of the Faust theme in a minor key. Hauke Haien, a bright and ambitious boy living in the previous century, grows up to become dikemaster in his seacoast village, the most prominent and responsible position it has to offer. From the start he is set off from his fellows by his energy, ability, and ambition. Each step of the way relations worsen between him and the rest of the traditionalistic, lethargic community. As dikemaster, he is finally in a position to fulfill his great ambition of building a new, modern dike of his own design that will reclaim hundreds of acres of land from the sea and long outlast the older, less durable dikes. This ambition becomes the ground on which he hopes to unite his personal interest with that of the community—an echo of Goethe's Faust, who, through his colonization project, seeks "On free soil to stand with a people free."

Under Hauke's stern leadership, the dike is built, but only over the discontent of the townspeople, who do not see their advantage in it, and who would rather have gone on repairing the old dikes and living in their old ways. They express their hostility by labeling Hauke, rightly, an atheist, and by circulating the rumor that a white horse he bought was actually the ghostly, devilish white horse of legend that was said to roam an offshore island. The completion of the dike leaves Hauke more isolated than ever, for which he compensates by becoming more obsessed with the dike than ever, thus appearing, in the eyes of the townspeople more devilish than ever. The climax comes when a terrible storm arises and the surging sea, representing the mysterious forces of destruction, bursts through just where the new dike adjoins the old, as if to suggest that tradition and innovation cannot coexist for long, that one must ultimately yield to the other. No one wins; Hauke's wife and child, the only humans he ever loved, are drowned, and the whole village is inundated. The denouement illustrates Storm's writing at its best:[21]

The moon shown down from on high. But below, on the dike, there was no more life. The wild water soon took possession of the whole reclaimed area. Hauke Haien's mound still jutted up from the rushing waves. The light still shone from his empty house. From the uplands, after the houses there had gradually darkened and vanished one after the other, the lonely fire in the church tower threw its flickering light over the boiling waves.

Storm passed no clear-cut judgments in this story. Both Hauke and the townspeople are given their due, but both are destroyed. No doubt his sympathies leaned in Hauke's direction, but with nothing like the confidence and assurance that Goethe had felt for his own Faust. As an artist and therefore an innovator himself, Storm could certainly feel something special for Hauke. The new dike is the only thing that survives the storm and endures. Also the fictitious narrator of the story, speaking for Storm, notes toward the end:[22]

You'll recall the prophecy made by old Jeve Manners so long ago: that a day would come when the grandchildren of the men then living would offer their gratitude to the builder of the dike. And, as you've seen, that day hasn't arrived. Not quite yet. Whatever the reason may be, sir, it's the way this world is built: men gave Socrates poison to drink, and then proceeded to nail Our Lord to the cross! During recent years, proceedings of that kind have become inconvenient. But we still make an official saint out of a cruel brute or a vicious, bull-necked priest. That is always popular.

The Rider on the White Horse touched on a vital issue of the day, in Germany and in Europe as a whole. But was not the real victor in the story the blind, furious force of nature? Was Storm saying that the confrontation between past and present must inevitably end in disaster? Was he saying that well enough should be left alone? Or was he saying that it ought and must give way to what is better, no matter what the cost? Storm could pose these questions, but not resolve them. This dilemma was the sign of his deep personal renunciation by default. In the end, the impartial reader is inclined to agree with the fictitious listener in the tale: "Well, we'll have to sleep on it."[23]

Theodor Fontane and *Effie Briest*

At the opposite end of the spectrum of renunciation from Storm was Fontane.[24] The novel, rather than the *Novelle*, was Fontane's medium, and, for him, "The novel should be a picture of the times to which we belong, or at least the reflection of the times adjacent to ours . . . ."[25] The series of novels, which he began to write late in life, at the age of sixty, are all characterized by accurate description, contemporaneity, and detachment; qualities he had acquired earlier as a journalist, traveler, and author of a four-volume travelog and social commentary, entitled *Journeys Through the Brandenburg Mark* (1862–1888). In all of his novels—*Errors, Entanglements* (1889), *Stine* (1890), *Frau Jenny Treibel* (1892), *Effie Briest* (1895), *The Poggenpuhls* (1896), and *The Stechlin* (1898)—the social types of the time emerge clearly and accurately defined and dominate the dramatic action. Starting as a reporter of the world around him, Fontane gradually became its leading literary analyst. Originally only a detached observer of Bismarckian Prussia, he emerged as its most astute interpreter and Germany's foremost social realist of the age.

Fontane was most concerned in his writings with the Prussian aristocracy, "those fellows who are intolerable and charming at the same time."[26] Temperamentally, he felt more akin to them than to any other class. "Who would abolish the nobility would abolish the last vestige of poetry in our world."[27] At the same time, Fontane, a provincial bourgeois himself, never believed that the Junker qualities he admired were confined to that class alone. "I solemnly protest against the fact," he writes, "that what I call noble is confined only to that class which is known as nobility. It is to be found in all classes. It means a sense of the common good, of the ideal, and an antipathy towards the triflings of a narrow and petty circle."[28] Moreover, Fontane had no illusions about the Junkers' sense of superiority, about their right and ability to rule, or their social justification for existence in the modern world. He was well aware of "the intolerant character of the Junkers," the naiveté of their "conviction of their exclusive right and capability to rule," and their "pseudo-conservatism, which in the long run is only based on egoism and on all that which is subservient to it."[29] He was equally well aware of the vitality and importance of the working classes, although he rarely dealt with them in his novels. In a letter to an English friend, he wrote:[30]

Only the fourth estate is interesting. The bourgeois is frightful, the nobility and church are behind the times, they never change. The new and better world begins only at the fourth estate. One would have to say this even if there were only very small signs of it. But such is not the case. What the workers think, write, and speak, has far outstripped the thinking, writing, and speaking of the traditionally ruling classes. Everything is more genuine, truer, more living. They, the workers, take hold of things in a new way. They have not only new goals, but new roads leading to them.

All of Fontane's writings explore the hold that social codes and conventions have on people's lives and their inability or unwillingness to violate them. In the exceptional case where someone attempts to do so, the result is either disappointment or disaster. If Fontane concentrated on the Prussian Junkers, it was not because he admired them above the other classes, but rather because their outmoded social codes and habits were comparatively more rigid and scrupulously adhered to, and therefore a more determinant factor in their lives. This class provided, therefore, a more fertile field for investigating the effects, both good and bad, but mostly bad, of social customs and conventions on human life. The Junker life-style was also the dominant one in Germany at the time, and therefore of greater social significance than the others. However, Fontane, although he wrote about and for the nobility, actually found his readership among the liberal middle classes, especially the liberal Berlin Jews, who played a commanding role in German cultural affairs at the time. And in none of his novels did Fontane handle his chosen theme with greater effect and insight than in *Effie Briest.*

Effie, the charming but unexceptional daughter of unexceptional Junker parents, unhesitatingly agrees to a proper but loveless marriage to the much older Baron von Innstetten, who is a successful government official and an exemplary representative of his class. After the marriage, they move to a provincial town, which Effie finds uninteresting and restrictive. Soon she also feels neglected by her unsentimental husband. More out of momentary boredom and listlessness than anything else, she yields to the advances of Major Crampas, a family friend. The affair is quickly over and forgotten, and the marriage continues thereafter on an even keel. Seven years later, Innstetten, by accident, learns of his wife's former infidelity.

At this point, the moral issues underlying the story thus far come to the fore. All the characters, including Effie herself, accept and respect the code of honor governing their class. On the other hand, they all possess human qualities capable of running counter to that code. Effie is, after all, charming, spontaneous, and emotionally alive. Innstetten, always kind and considerate toward her, realizes how deeply he cares for her, even after he discovers her infidelity. And Effie's respectable parents love her enough finally to violate the social code and take her in after her husband has cast her out. The collision between these human qualities and the social code dominates the closing chapters. Innstetten hesitates before challenging Crampas to a duel, and, in a chapter that one critic calls the "greatest conversation scene in the German novel," [31] these two sides of his character confront each other: [32]

We are not merely individuals, we belong to a whole, and have always to take the whole into consideration. We are absolutely dependent. If it were possible to live in solitude I could let it pass. I should then bear the burden heaped upon me, though real happiness would be gone. But so many people are forced to live without real happiness, and I should have to do it too, and I could. We don't need to be happy, least of all have we any claim on happiness, and it is not absolutely necessary to put out of existence the one who has taken our happiness away. We can let him go, if we desire to live on apart from the world. But in the social life of the world a certain something has been worked out that is now in force, and in accordance with the principles of which we have been accustomed to judge everybody, ourselves as well as others. It would never do to run counter to it. Society would despise us and in the end we should despise ourselves and, not being able to bear the strain, we should fire a bullet into our brains.

Innstetten's alter ego, Wüllersdorf, who had originally urged him to drop the matter and go on with Effie as before, now echoes his thoughts:[33]

I think it is awful that you should be right, but you are *right. I shall no longer trouble you with my "must it be." The world is simply as it is, and things do not take the course we desire, but the one others desire. This talk about the "ordeal," with which many pompous orators seek to assure us, is sheer nonsense, there is nothing in it. On the contrary, our cult of honor is idolatry, but we must submit to it so long as the idol is honored.*

After the duel, in which Innstetten kills Crampas, the matter is still not resolved in his mind:[34]

When we carry a thing to extremes we carry it too far and make ourselves ridiculous. No doubt about it. But where does it begin? Where is the limit? Within ten years a duel is required and we call it an affair of honor. After eleven years, or perhaps ten and a half, we call it nonsense. The limit, the limit. Where is it? Was it reached? Was it passed? . . . Now if I had been full of deadly hatred, if a deep feeling of revenge had found a place in my heart—Revenge is not a thing of beauty, but a human trait and has naturally a human right to exist. But this affair was all for the sake of an idea, a conception, was artificial, half comedy. And now I must continue this comedy, must send Effie away and ruin her, and myself, too.

When, in pain and remorse, Innstetten decides to dash off to Africa, exclaiming: "For culture and honor are to blame for all my trouble," Wüllersdorf advises him: "Simply stay and practice resignation. . . . The best thing is to stand in the gap and hold out till one falls, but, until then, to get as much out of life as possible in the small and even the smallest things. . . ."[35] As for Effie, she is now cast out and disgraced, attended only by her simple maid

Roswitha, who stands by her until the end, which comes quickly. On meeting her daughter, whom she has not seen for some time, and whom Innstetten has turned against her, Effie reflects:[36]

I thought he had a noble heart and have always felt small beside him, but now I know that it is he who is small. And because he is small he is cruel. Everything that is small is cruel. . . . Honor, honor, honor. And then he shot the poor fellow whom I never even loved and whom I had forgotten, because I didn't love him.

At the point of death, however, she reconsiders: "He has much that is good in his nature and was as noble as anybody can be who is not truly in love."[37]

In this novel, which is in a class with *Madame Bovary* and *Anna Karenina,* Fontane succeeded in diagnosing, with deadly accuracy and superb artistry, the paramount human dilemma instrinsic to the life-style of Germany's ruling classes in the time of Bismarck. In the end the social code wins out; almost inexorably, it seems, and to everyone's misfortune. Nothing emerges from *Effie Briest* so clearly as the pathos and pathology of a defunct social class so insecure that it must cling, come hell or high water, to a tribal code, which is destructive and even self-destructive, in order to justify its existence and find honor and meaning in life. But, for all the accuracy of Fontane's assessment and his ability to express it artistically, and for all his sensitivity to the real movement and direction of history, no alternative to adherence to such a code, explicit or otherwise, emerges from his writing. Neither Emma Bovary, who is Effie's inferior as a human type, nor Anna Karenina, who is her superior, are as submissive as she to a social ethic, which in the end destroys them all. Fontane did not, of course, sanction the Junker ethic; but, then, he did not effectively oppose it either. In *Errors, Entanglements,* the hero concludes: "Many things are allowed but we must keep clear of what strikes deep; keep hearts out of it, even if it were only your own that is involved."[38] And in *The Stechlin,* Fontane's last novel, one of the leading characters, Dubslav, restates this view: "To accept the law in peace and resignation, that is what makes a man moral and raises him up."[39] In contrast to Storm, who found resignation in withdrawal from the world and in inwardness, Fontane, tolerant, compassionate, but realistic, found it through acquiescence in the world as given.

Burckhardt and Nietzsche: The Devaluation of History

*By the word "unhistorical" I mean the power, the
art, of forgetting and of drawing a limited horizon
round oneself. I call the power "superhistorical"*

which turns the eyes from the process of becoming to
that which gives existence an eternal and stable
character—to art and religion.

Nietzsche

Of the major German historians of the second half of the century, the one most sensitive to the discontinuity between past and present, and its adverse effects on culture and society, was the conservative Swiss humanist Jakob Burckhardt (1818–1897). As a devoted citizen of tiny Switzerland, a country at the juncture of three major European cultures, but far removed from the political power struggles involving the rest of Europe, Burckhardt was naturally inclined toward cosmopolitanism and aloofness from the nationalism rampant elsewhere, especially in Germany. From this vantage point he did more than any other historian of his time to promote cultural history, an approach to the past deliberately designed to counteract the excessive preoccupation among historians with political and national history, and one that came to thrive, understandably, in other small countries, like Holland and the Scandinavian states, which no longer played a leading role in European political affairs.

But Burckhardt was also educated in Germany, and whether he found Germany admirable, as in his youth, or disgusting, as he did in later life, he always moved within the German intellectual sphere. Early in life he stated an opinion, in reference to what he thought at the time Switzerland's cultural relationship to Germany should be, that would characterize his later attitude toward history in general: "There is only one remedy against the threatening decline of a people, and that is: to renew its links with its origins."[40] For, as the scion of an old, prominent patrician family of Basle, noted for its contributions through the generations to the civic and cultural life of that city, Burckhardt was in a good position to sense the threat to his traditionalistic way of life posed by the advent of modernization. And in the cultural life of pre-1848 Germany, which was still closely linked with that of Switzerland, he thought he saw the means to combat it. Burckhardt's Basle was not unlike Henry Adams' Boston. Both cities, with strong patriarchal traditions and institutions, were unusually resistant to modernization; and both men, with deep personal roots in those traditions, felt acutely out of place in the dawning new age of machines and mass society. Dispossessed of their past and distrustful of the present, both personified in their own lives the historical transition, by which the social class of their origins was being victimized, and which they in turn attempted to interpret intellectually from similar standpoints.

Burckhardt had all the makings—the background and desire,

the temperament and talent—to be an articulate spokesman for a refined conservatism. He became that, and more besides. For history was more to him than a source of knowledge or inspiration, and more than a means of escape from the present, which were still popular justifications for the study of history. In Burckhardt's hands, history became an eloquent personal and intellectual instrument with which to denounce the age. Not surprisingly, he was drawn to periods of rapid transition, in which the breakdown of long-standing social and spiritual traditions was making way for the emergence of a new creative elite. His two greatest works, *The Age of Constantine* (1852) and *The Culture of the Italian Renaissance* (1860), both reflected his view that civilization, man's noblest achievement, is a fragile creation that must be constantly defended by an educated elite against the destructiveness of the ever ignorant and indifferent masses. For Burckhardt, history was not, therefore, the story of the steady progress of mankind, but rather a constant tension and alternation between the purely creative forces of culture, as represented by the gifted few, and the anticreative forces, represented by the philistine majority. This conception gained momentum in German thinking as the century progressed, appearing in Ferdinand Tönnies (1855–1936) as a dichotomy between Community and Society, in Oswald Spengler (1880–1936) as a tension between Culture and Civilization, and in Thomas Mann (1875–1955) as a tension between Spirit and Life. "Something great, new, and liberating must come out of Germany," Burckhardt wrote to a friend in 1872, "and what is more *in opposition to* power, wealth, and business; it will have to have its martyrs; it must be something which of its very nature will swim above water and survive political, economic, and other catastrophes."[41]

Burckhardt departed from the main current of German historical thought in another respect also. He rejected any philosophical systematization of history whatever, whether in the manner of Hegel, Ranke, the liberals, or the nationalists. "The interpretation of the facts is going through a complete and thorough molt," he wrote after Prussia's victory over France, "and one will have to wait some years before the history of the world, beginning with Adam, has been painted in victorious German colors and orientated towards 1870 and 1871."[42] And elsewhere: "The philosophy of history is a centaur, a contradiction in terms, for history coordinates, and hence is unphilosophical, while philosophy subordinates, and hence is unhistorical."[43]

Burckhardt's aim, of course, was to expose and warn against the distortion of history and its utilization as an instrument of ideological or political propaganda. From the premise that philosophy and history are mutually exclusive, which was itself a philosophical proposition, he logically concluded that history can have nothing to do with beginnings and ends, that history contains no meaning, whether transcendental or immanent, and that progress is a concept alien to real history. In taking this position, however, Burckhardt deprived himself of any justification for the study of history other than a purely subjective and aesthetic one. To his brilliant young admirer, Friedrich Nietzsche, he confided:[44]

I never dreamt of training scholars and disciples in the narrower sense, but only wanted to make every member of my audience feel and know that everyone may and must appropriate those aspects of the past which appeal to him personally, and that there may be happiness in so doing.

Thus, Burckhardt's denunciation of the intellectual currents of his time actually served to sanction, albeit indirectly and inadvertently, the very views and values of those whom he opposed. Although he disliked Ranke, he shared Ranke's conservative outlook. For only that which survives the vicissitudes of time seemed to him worthy of the historian's attention, since his definition of history excluded any supposedly unhistorical idea of general progress. He disliked Bismarck, but he left himself no choice except to regard him as inevitable.[45]

Bismarck has only taken into his own hands what would have happened in due course without him and in opposition to him. He saw that the growing wave of social-democracy would somehow or other bring about a state of naked power, whether through the democrats themselves, or through the governments, and said: Ipse faciam, *and embarked on three wars, 1864, 1866, 1870.*

He disliked Wagner for his excessive nationalism, but he was prepared to believe that "Europe's greatest insurance . . . against war—and let us still hope, for peace—is the German army."[46] He disliked liberals and Jews for their excessive materialism and optimism, but his own brand of pessimism, which was perfectly consistent with passive positivism, provided little with which to combat these tendencies, which he considered inevitable anyway. His own best hope was "that the crisis may suddenly pass from the contemptible field of 'property and gain' on to quite another and that then the 'right man' may appear overnight—and all the world will follow in his train."[47]

Burckhardt found a disciple in Friedrich Nietzsche (1844–1900), who was temperamentally and intellectually his opposite, but quick to grasp the implications of his "unphilosophical" approach to history.[48] Nietzsche arrived in Basle from Germany in 1869, where he taught at the university for the next ten years alongside the older, mild-mannered professor. Under Burckhardt's influence, Nietzsche began to develop his characteristic views on history that would later play an important part in his overall philosophy. He was attracted to Burckhardt's cultural and elitist conception of history. And Nietzsche's essay *The Use and Abuse of History* (1873) echoed Burckhardt's view that history has no intrinsic meaning or ultimate purpose, but serves rather to show how incompatible the past and present are. Both men sought to discredit the use of history, particularly in Germany, as a means to justify a society they despised. In doing so, however, each developed a theory of history that precluded the possibility of reconciling the past and present. But, whereas Burckhardt chose to immerse himself in the past, holding up the greatness he found in it as an indictment of the age, Nietzsche drew the opposite conclusion from the same premise. For him, an excessive interest in the past is precisely what poisons the present, makes it an unworthy heir to its own best traditions:[49]

An excess of history seems to be an enemy to the life of a time, and dangerous in five ways. Firstly, the contrast of inner and outer is emphasized and personality weakened. Secondly, the time comes to imagine that it possesses the rarest of virtues, justice, to a higher degree than any other time. Thirdly, the instincts of a nation are thwarted, the maturity of the individual arrested no less than that of the whole. Fourthly, we get the belief in the old age of mankind, the belief, at all times, harmful, that we are late survivals, mere epigoni. Lastly, an age reaches a dangerous condition of irony with regard to itself, and the still more dangerous state of cynicism, when a cunning egoistic theory of action is matured that maims and at last destroys the vital strength.

In his first important writing, *The Birth of Tragedy* (1872), Nietzsche, like so many German thinkers and poets before him, turned to the Greek experience as a guide to the development of his ideas about culture and society in general. This work bears the traces of Nietzsche's deep admiration at the time for Hölderlin's poetry, Schopenhauer's philosophy, Wagner's music, as well as Burckhardt's view of history. It attempts to explain the rise of Greek tragedy as a momentary reconciliation of two antagonistic life forces or principles, which Nietzsche termed the Dionysiac and Apollonian. The Dionysiac is the spirit of music and will, instinct and ecstasy, the irrational and mythical, vitality and nature in all its formless dynamism and immediacy. Opposed to it is the visual Apollonian principle, representing order and form, reason and measure, the stable and static. The genius of the Greeks was their ability to unite the two for a time in the form of tragedy, which Nietzsche characterized as "an Apollonian embodiment of Dionysiac insights and powers. . . ."[50] Greek tragedy began to decline when the Apollonian, personified in real life by the intellectualistic and optimistic Socrates, gained the upper hand over the Dionysiac and succeeded in suppressing it. "Once that optimistic [Socratic] element had entered tragedy, it overgrew its Dionysiac regions and brought about their annihilation and, finally, the leap into genteel domestic drama." [51] Or, again:[52]

Understanding kills action, for in order to act we require the veil of illusion; such is Hamlet's doctrine, not to be confounded with the cheap wisdom of John-a-Dreams, who through too much reflection, as it were a surplus of possibilities, never arrives at action. What, both in the case of Hamlet and Dionysiac man, overbalances any motive leading to action, is not reflection but understanding, the apprehension of truth and its terror.

Nietzsche's bold interpretation of tragedy represented a direct assault on the older German classical conception of the Greeks, which German scholars of the Bismarck era were still inclined to accept. The viewpoint that had developed from Winckelmann to Schiller, Nietzsche believed, had exaggerated the Apollonian aspects of Greek civilization at the expense of its Dionysiac traits. Serenity, stability, and simplicity had not been characteristic of the Greeks, he maintained; their civilization had not been notably harmonious and balanced, nor had the Greeks themselves actually lived the sort of ideal life they had accorded to their gods. On the contrary, the Greeks, like all peoples throughout history, had been beset by complexity and tension, strain and suffering, fear and uncertainty, all of which they had sought to master by spiritual means:[53]

The Greeks were keenly aware of the terrors and horrors of existence; in order to be able to live at all they had to place before them the shining fantasy of the Olympians. Their tremendous distrust of the titanic forces of nature: Moira, mercilessly enthroned beyond the knowable world; the vulture which fed upon the great philanthropist Prometheus; the terrible lot drawn by wise Oedipus; the curse on the house of Atreus which brought Orestes to the murder of his mother: that whole Panic philosophy, in short, with its mythic examples, by which the gloomy Etruscans perished, the Greeks conquered—or at least hid from view—again and again by means of this artificial Olympus. In order to live at all the Greeks had to construct these deities.

Nietzsche's view was, in certain respects, a bracing antidote to the idealization of the Greeks by the German classicists. They had simply ascribed to the Greeks all those desirable (Apollonian) human qualities they missed in modern life and wished to see restored. In doing so, however, they not only had distorted historical reality; they had also defeated their purpose by effectively widening, rather than diminishing, the gulf separating modern from ancient life. By contrast, Nietzsche's theory implied that the essential forces operative in ancient Greece were the same forces operative among all men everywhere and always. What the Greeks achieved, briefly, in tragedy—the unity of conflicting timeless principles—is potentially within the reach of any society that wills it. In diametrical contrast to the classical view, Nietzsche held that the Greeks had achieved this ideal unity by giving free reign to the Dionysiac spirit, and that modern man fails to achieve it because he allows the Apollonian to smother the Dionysiac—a view that already pointed in the direction of Freud. However, in criticizing the exaggeration of the Apollonian spirit in the classical interpretation of the Greeks, Nietzsche reacted in the opposite direction. In *The Birth of Tragedy* he says much about the ill effects of an excess of intellect and science on culture and on human life in general, but, typically, nothing about the ill effects of an excess of instinct and passion. "Amidst our degenerate culture music is the only pure and purifying flame, towards which and away from which all things move in a Heracleitean double motion. All that is now called culture, education, civilization will one day have to appear before the incorruptible judge, Dionysos."[54]

Nietzsche, like the classicists, used the Greeks as a stick with which to beat modern society. Only, for him, the defect of modern man, of modern German man especially, was his submission to the Apollonian; a defect that could be remedied, he believed, only by a return to the primordial fount of myth. A return to the Greeks he equated with a return to irrationality. "Every culture that has lost myth has lost, by the same token, its natural creativity."[55] In all this Nietzsche shared the presuppositions of others discussed in this chapter. Like Burckhardt, Nietzsche conceived history not as the story of human progress but as an endless, essentially meaningless struggle between the elitist forces of culture and the philistine forces of anticulture. With Schopenhauer he held a strongly pessimistic view of the world, according to which man is driven by the blind, insatiable force of will. With Wagner he held that the mobilization of the Dionysiac, by means of music from which it had originated, was the only way to restore myth to its rightful primary role in the life of German society:[56]

Let no one believe that the German spirit has irrevocably lost its Dionysiac home so long as those bird voices can clearly be heard telling of that home. One day the knight will awaken, in all the morning freshness of his long sleep. He will slay dragons, destroy the cunning dwarfs, rouse Brünnhilde, and not even Wotan's spear will be able to bar his way.

It is true that, later in life, Nietzsche revised his opinion of Schopenhauer and Wagner. Even then, however, he did not abandon the premises of their thinking, but only their conclusions. As against Schopenhauer's advocacy of withdrawal into aesthetic quiescence as a way to escape the suffering and absurdity of the world, Nietzsche came to advocate an attitude of acceptance and enjoyment of the world. He still held that the world is essentially absurd, but he now concluded that its absurdity is no reason to reject the world. As a step in the development of his theory of the superman, and in anticipation of existentialism, Nietzsche came to regard the meaninglessness of existence, since it cannot be changed, as a sanction for rejoicing in it. In 1876 Nietzsche also broke off his close friendship with Wagner and turned against him. Nietzsche still believed in the idea of reactivating myth by means of music, but he now believed that Wagner, who had suddenly become famous and correspondingly well disposed toward the new *Reich,* was more concerned with pandering to popular taste and propagating Bismarckian ideals than with following through his original artistic objective.

These developments, therefore, did not substantially alter Nietzsche's views as they emerged in his later writings, *Thus Spake Zarathustra* (1883–1885) and *The Genealogy of Morals* (1887). In these works Nietzsche carried to its extreme the century-long trend in German thought to envision civilization and culture as polar opposites, the first wholly negative and the second wholly positive. *The Genealogy of Morals* was, for its time, a daring, devastating inquiry into the origins and role of morality in history. It depicts morality, the foundation of civilization, as a creation of the weak and incompetent, the resentful and dissatisfied of this world: "the slaves, the mob, the herd, whatever else you wish to call them." [57] Morality emerges here as the product of a socio- and psychopathological development in history; an ascetic ideal, which Nietzsche describes as "this hatred of humanity, of animality, of inert matter; this loathing of the senses, of reason even; this fear of beauty and happiness; this longing to escape from illusion, change, becoming, death, and from longing itself. It signifies, let us have the courage to face it, a will to nothingness, a revulsion from life, a rebellion against the principal conditions of living." [58]

Unalterably opposed to (civilized) moral man is the (cultured) superman, who is the subject of *Thus Spake Zarathustra.* The line of thought, begun in *The Birth of Tragedy,* culminates here in the doctrines of the will to power, the transvaluation of all values, and eternal recurrence. All were intended to fill the spiritual void left by Nietzsche's earlier devaluation of historical man. "Man is a rope stretched between the animal and the Superman—a rope over an abyss. . . . What is great in man is that he is a bridge and not a goal." [59] The extreme fatalism of the theory of eternal recurrence, a restatement of the ancient idea of history as an endless, inevitable succession of cycles, was intended by Nietzsche to deprive contemporary man of the past as a crutch, a comfort, or a justification for existence. The only solace of this doctrine is the opportunity it affords the individual to live his life so that it will be worthy of infinite repetitions. "To redeem what is past, and to transform every 'It was' into 'Thus would I have it!'—that only do I call redemption!'[60] Since the meaninglessness of the past disqualifies it to be a guide to the present, the worthy life—like that of Nietzsche's mythologized Zarathustra—must be lived in solitary defiance of the world, which is little more than the passive product of the past. For Nietzsche, this meant a sweeping rejection of all merely historical values, especially moral values, which do little but suppress physical and spiritual vitality. Nihilism and creativity are but two sides of the same coin. Rejection of history is the prerequisite of creativity, and creativity the fruit of man's liberation from the past. This is what Nietzsche meant by the transvaluation of all values and the will to power, which is the work of the rare superman.

Nietzsche's view of life was, by his own admission, a tragic one. For the superman must live in the recognition that his existence, like everyone else's, is part of a fatalistic cycle; an existence enacted in earlier cycles and destined to be reenacted in later ones. "Behold, we know what thou teachest: that all things eternally return, and ourselves with them, and that we have already existed times without number, and all things with us."[61] The superman must also live in the recognition that his titanic efforts to transform himself and the world can have little effect, since all that has been, is and ever will be, although in constantly changing forms and manifestations. By virtue of being a superman, therefore, he cannot and does not expect to be understood or heeded by his inferior fellowmen. "Oh, how sad the buffoons of the populace seem today! This today, however, is that of the populace."[62] "Before the populace, however, we will not be equal. Ye higher men, away from the market-place!"[63] Precisely because of this unbridgeable gulf, as Nietzsche saw it, between the superman and the rest of society, his fierce denunciation of the age, like that of Burckhardt and others of the time, was bound to go down in defeat. As one recent commentator said of Nietzsche:[64]

The terrible truth was simply this. He was not the prophet of a new and glorious age; he was one of the last great forces of a world which was dying in Europe when he wrote. . . . His vision of the re-birth of tragedy and a new heroic age was a wish-dream, the self-intoxication not of a prophet but of a martyr; of a great decadent (he knew it himself) in whom the unearthly hopes of Hölderlin fought the tragic despair of Heine.

At the very moment when Central Europe was finally being swept into the current of modernization, Germany's foremost thinker was formulating a philosophy designed to enable the individual to resist and cut himself adrift from that current. Nietzsche's view of life was tragic because it was incapable of serving as a call to action. Rather, it signified the typical predicament of the

German intelligentsia throughout the century: its inability either to accept historical reality or to offer a feasible alternative to it. This inability in turn testified to the larger tragedy of a people who could neither accept nor avoid entry into the modern world.

Notes to Chapter Eight

1. See Henry C. Meyer, *Mitteleuropa in German Thought and Action, 1815–1945* (The Hague: Nijhoff, 1955), pp. 30–33.
2. Pinson, *op. cit.*, p. 121.
3. See Fritz Stern, *The Politics of Cultural Despair: A Study in the Rise of the Germanic Ideology* (Garden City, N.Y.: Doubleday, 1965).
4. *Ibid.*, p. 101.
5. See the essays on Wagner in Thomas Mann, *Essays of Three Decades*, trans. by H. T. Lowe-Porter (New York: Knopf, 1948). Also Jacques Barzun, *Darwin, Marx, Wagner,* 2nd rev. ed. (Garden City, N.Y.: Doubleday, 1958), Chapter 3; and Robert Raphael, *Richard Wagner* (New York: Twayne, 1969).
6. Mann, *ibid.*, p. 359.
7. Quoted in Raphael, *op. cit.*, p. 77.
8. Paul Lang, as quoted in Raphael, *ibid.*, p. 123.
9. William J. Bossenbrook, *The German Mind* (Detroit: Wayne State University Press, 1961), p. 348.
10. Fritz Stern, *op. cit.*, p. 7.
11. See Fritz Martini, *Deutsche Literatur im Bürgerlichen Realismus, 1848–1898* (Stuttgart: Metzler, 1962).
12. Quoted in Mann, *op. cit.*, p. 290.
13. *Ibid.*, p. 276.
14. *Loc. cit.*
15. Introduction to *Selected Stories by Theodor Storm*, ed. and trans. by James Wright (New York: Signet, 1964).
16. W. F. Mainland, "Theodor Storm," in *German Men of Letters*, ed. by Alex Natan (London: Wolff, 1961), p. 158.
17. Quoted in Roy Pascal, *The German Novel* (London: Methuen, 1965), p. 157.
18. Quoted in James Wright's introduction to *Selected Stories by Theodor Storm, op. cit.*, p. xv.
19. *Loc. cit.*
20. See Walter Silz, *Realism and Reality: Studies in the German Novelle of Poetic Realism* (Chapel Hill: University of North Carolina Press, 1954), Chapter 9.
21. *Selected Stories by Theodor Storm, op. cit.*, p. 282.
22. *Ibid.*, p. 283.
23. *Ibid.*, p. 284.
24. See Mann, *op. cit.*, Chapter 11; Pascal, *op. cit.*, Chapter 8; H. B. Garland, "Theodor Fontane," in *German Men of Letters, op. cit.*, Chapter 10; Joseph P. Stern, *Reinterpretations: Seven Studies in Nineteenth-Century German Literature* (New York: Basic Books, 1964), Chapter 7; Georg Lukács, *Deutsche Realisten des Neunzehnten Jahrhunderts* (Bern: Francke, 1951), Chapter 8; and Konrad Wandrey, *Theodor Fontane* (Munich: Beck, 1919).
25. Quoted in Pascal, *op. cit.*, p. 182.
26. Quoted in Ernest K. Bramsted, *Aristocracy and Middle Classes in Germany: Social Types in German Literature, 1830–1900,* rev. ed. (Chicago: University of Chicago Press, 1964), p. 265.
27. *Ibid.*, p. 264.
28. *Loc. cit.*
29. *Ibid.*, p. 265.
30. Quoted in Mann, *op. cit.*, p. 302.

31. Wandrey, *op. cit.*, p. 285.
32. Theodor Fontane, *Effie Briest,* trans. by W. A. Cooper (New York: Ungar, 1966), p. 179.
33. *Ibid.*, p. 181.
34. *Ibid.*, p. 187.
35. *Ibid.*, pp. 226–227.
36. *Ibid.*, p. 213.
37. *Ibid.*, p. 233.
38. Quoted in Garland, *op. cit.*, p. 283.
39. Quoted in Joseph P. Stern, *op. cit.*, p. 347.
40. Letter to Louise Burckhardt, September 25, 1841 in *The Letters of Jacob Burckhardt,* ed. and trans. by Alexander Dru (New York: Pantheon, 1955), p. 65.
41. Letter to Arnold von Salis, April 21, 1872, *ibid.*, p. 151.
42. Letter to Friedrich von Preen, December 31, 1872, *ibid.*, p. 157.
43. *Force and Freedom: An Interpretation of History by Jacob Burckhardt,* ed. by J. H. Nichols (New York: Meridian, 1955), p. 72.
44. Letter of February 25, 1874 in *The Letters of Jacob Burckhardt, op. cit.*, p. 158.
45. Letter to Friedrich von Preen, April 26, 1872, *ibid.*, p. 151.
46. Letter to Friedrich von Preen, October 15, 1887, *ibid.*, p. 215.
47. *Force and Freedom, op. cit.*, p. 306.
48. See Alfred von Martin, *Nietzsche und Burckhardt,* 4th ed. (Munich: Erasmus, 1947); George A. Morgan, *What Nietzsche Means* (Cambridge, Mass.: Harvard University Press, 1941); and Frank A. Lea, *The Tragic Philosopher: A Study of Friedrich Nietzsche* (London: Methuen, 1957).
49. Friedrich Wilhelm Nietzsche, *The Use and Abuse of History,* trans. by A. Collins (New York: Liberal Arts Library, 1957), p. 28.
50. Friedrich Wilhelm Nietzsche, *"The Birth of Tragedy,"* trans. by F. Golffing (Garden City, N.Y.: Doubleday Anchor, 1956), pp. 56–57.
51. *Ibid.*, p. 88.
52. *Ibid.*, p. 51.
53. *Ibid.*, pp. 29–30.
54. *Ibid.*, p. 120.
55. *Ibid.*, p. 136.
56. *Ibid.*, p. 144.
57. *Ibid.*, p. 169.
58. *Ibid.*, p. 299.
59. Friedrich Wilhelm Nietzsche, *Thus Spake Zarathustra,* trans. by T. Common in *The Philosophy of Nietzsche* (New York: Modern Library, 1954), p. 8.
60. *Ibid.*, p. 153.
61. *Ibid.*, p. 247.
62. *Ibid.*, p. 331.
63. *Ibid.*, p. 320.
64. E. M. Butler, *The Tyranny of Greece over Germany,* 2nd ed. (Boston: Beacon, 1958), p. 313.

CONCLUSION

Germany in the age of Bismarck was a society in the last phase of rapid transition from a traditionalistic to a modern order. It was a society in which the continuity of historical development had broken down sufficiently to prevent Germans from being able to relate easily and meaningfully to their past, but not sufficiently to enable them to evolve new institutions, values, and patterns of social and personal conduct appropriate to their new situation. No amount of knowledge of the political, social, and economic realities alone of this era can fully reveal the intense strains and internal tensions to which Germans were subject at this point in their development, and to which they had been subject throughout the process leading up to it. The vast majority of Germans were satisfied with Bismarck's accomplishments and proud of Germany's newly won power and prestige. They were little concerned about the drastic upheaval in political and social, moral and intellectual attitudes involved in this process. The few who were greatly concerned, the critical and inquiring, found themselves in the main relegated to the periphery of German life at this time, which was itself a new and significant by-product of the period.

To all appearances, the new German *Reich* was a going concern. True, it was a society inconsistent with its own historical traditions as well as with the ideals and institutions that had stimulated modernization in the West; a society therefore that lacked the sanction of both the past and present. True, this society represented a haphazard conglomeration of old revived feudal remnants and new middle-class bureaucratic elements, and an uneasy balance between many other mutually hostile social forces. True, the state interests of Prussia and the national interests of Germany as a whole often conflicted with each other. True, also, that the lofty human ideals, proclaimed by classicism, romanticism, and idealism during the early stages of Germany's transition, rapidly gave way after 1848 to attitudes of pessimism and irrationality, accommodation and acquiescence. The appearance and reality of Bismarckian Germany, therefore, were not one and the same.

It was the best of Germany's intelligentsia who were most concerned with, and who gave clearest expression to, this discrepancy and its effects. Opposed to the declining old order, which had always been hostile to their progressive humanistic views, they also found themselves in conflict with the emerging new order, which regarded them at first as dangerous and then, with its consolidation of power and success, as irrelevant. The unsettling process of transition had deprived them of their traditional role in society, but had failed to provide them with any new role. By the time of Bismarck, Germany's best poets and thinkers could count themselves among her most dislocated and dysfunctional social elements. Not surprisingly, they responded, throughout the century, with increasing hostility toward the course of Germany's modernization in particular and toward modernization in general. In the process, since their very existence as artists and thinkers depended upon it, they entered into a searching and fruitful exploration of what the role and purpose of culture in the modern world, and what the relationship of the creative individual to it, can and ought to be.

The result of this exploration was a burst of critical and creative energy that raised Germany for a time to a position of leadership in European intellectual and cultural life. This ferment ran its course in the three broad phases examined above: self-redefinition, despair, and rejection. Goethe and Schiller, Kleist and Hoffmann, Kant and Hegel, Büchner and Heine, Schopenhauer and Marx, Storm and Fontane, Wagner, Burckhardt, and Nietzsche—these foremost representatives of the various phases of Germany's great age were only a few of the many brilliant nineteenth-century German interpreters of the proper relationship between culture and society. Their social dislocation, isolation, and lack of clearly defined interests and commitments provided the stimulus to their creative encounter with this problem. But these very conditions, which had produced the problem in the first place, were the same which precluded a solution to it. Alienation, a term Germans of the early nineteenth century were the first to use in its modern sense, gave rise to the peculiarly modern conception of culture as a critical mirror, as the *consciousness* of society, not merely its reflection or ideal or justification for existence. Historically, the two, alienation of the intellectual and culture thus conceived, went hand in hand.

These circumstances, although not confined to Germany, were more pronounced there than elsewhere. Nowhere else did the intellectual stand in such a strained relationship to the rest of society. Nowhere else did belief in the intrinsic and inevitable conflict between culture and civilization, community and society, spirit and life, thought and action gain such widespread acceptance. Nowhere else did reality seem so unacceptable to the intellectual and his ideals so unattainable. And nowhere else did the conception of culture as the consciousness of a society gone astray take such deep hold as in Germany. It fed back into the West, whence it had originally found inspiration, and filtered into Eastern Europe and elsewhere where modernization was just beginning to make itself felt. This conception of culture was the expression of a society contending desperately, but not very successfully, with problems that were rapidly becoming universal. But it proved to be Germany's most original and significant legacy to the rest of the world and to the very concept of modern culture.

BIBLIOGRAPHY

General Works

BARRACLOUGH, GEOFFREY. *The Origins of Modern German History*, 6th ed. New York: Capricorn, 1963.

BOSSENBROOK, WILLIAM J. *The German Mind*. Detroit: Wayne State University Press, 1961.

GOOCH, GEORGE P. *Studies in German History*. London: Longman's & Green, 1948.

HOLBORN, HAJO. *A History of Modern Germany*. 3 vols. New York: Knopf, 1959–1969.

KOHN, HANS. *The Mind of Germany*, rev. ed. New York: Harper, 1965.

MANN, GOLO. *The History of Germany Since 1789*. Trans. by M. JACKSON. New York: Praeger, 1968.

PINSON, KOPPEL S. *Modern Germany: Its History and Civilization*, 2nd ed. New York: Macmillan, 1966.

PLESSNER, HELMUTH. *Die Verspätete Nation*. Stuttgart: Kohlhammer, 1959.

REINHARDT, KURT F. *Germany: 2000 Years*, rev. ed. 2 vols. New York: Ungar, 1950–1961.

SCHNABEL, FRANZ. *Deutsche Geschichte im Neunzehnten Jahrhundert*, 5th ed. 4 vols. Freiburg im Breisgau: Herder, 1959.

SCHÜSSLER, WILHELM. *Um das Geschichtsbild*. Freizeiten: Gladbeck, 1953.

SIMON, WALTER M. *Germany: A Brief History*. New York: Random House, 1966.

STADELMANN, RUDOLF. *Deutschland und Westeuropa*. Württemberg: Steiner, 1948.

VERMEIL, EDMOND. *L'Allemagne, Essai d'Explication*, 3rd ed. Paris: Gallimard, 1945.

Specific Topics

BARTH, KARL. *Protestant Thought: From Rousseau to Ritschl*. Trans. by B. COZENS. New York: Harper, 1959.

BOESCHENSTEIN, HERMANN. *German Literature of the Nineteenth Century*. London: Arnold, 1969.

BRAMSTED, ERNEST K. *Aristocracy and Middle Classes in Germany: Social Types in German Literature, 1830–1900*, rev. ed. Chicago: University of Chicago Press, 1964.

BUTLER, ELIZA M. *The Tyranny of Greece over Germany*, 2nd ed. Boston: Beacon, 1958.

CLAPHAM, J. H. *The Economic Development of France and Germany*, 4th ed. Cambridge, England: The University Press, 1966.

CRAIG, GORDON A. *The Politics of the Prussian Army, 1640–1945.* Oxford: Clarendon, 1955.

HAMBURGER, MICHAEL. *Reason and Energy: Studies in German Literature.* New York: Grove, 1957.

HAMEROW, THEODORE S. *Restoration, Revolution, Reaction: Economics and Politics in Germany, 1815–1871.* Princeton, N.J.: Princeton University Press, 1966.

HELLER, ERICH. *The Disinherited Mind.* New York: Meridian, 1959.

IGGERS, GEORG G. *The German Conception of History.* Middletown, Conn.: Wesleyan University Press, 1968.

KEDOURIE, ELIE. *Nationalism,* rev. ed. New York: Praeger, 1960.

KOHN, HANS (ed.). *German History: Some New German Views.* Boston: Beacon, 1954.

KRIEGER, LEONARD. *The German Idea of Freedom.* Boston: Beacon, 1957.

LILGE, FREDERIC. *The Abuse of Learning: The Failure of the German University.* New York: Macmillan, 1948.

LIPTZIN, SOLOMON. *Historical Survey of German Literature: From Novalis to Nietzsche.* New York: Prentice-Hall, 1936.

————. *Germany's Stepchildren.* Cleveland and New York: World Publishing Co., 1961.

LÖWITH, KARL. *From Hegel to Nietzsche: The Revolution in Nineteenth-Century Thought,* 3rd rev. ed. Trans. by D. E. GREEN. London: Constable, 1965.

LÚKACS, GEORG. *Deutsche Realisten des Neunzehnten Jahrhunderts.* Bern: Francke, 1951.

————. *Die Zerstörung der Vernunft.* Neuwied am Rhein: Luchterhand, 1962.

MANN, THOMAS. *Essays of Three Decades.* Trans. by H. T. LOWE-PORTER. New York: Knopf, 1948.

MARCUSE, HERBERT. *Reason and Revolution,* 2nd ed. Boston: Beacon, 1960.

MAYER, HANS. *Von Lessing bis Thomas Mann.* Württemberg: Neske, 1959.

MEINECKE, FRIEDRICH. *Cosmopolitanism and the National State.* Trans. by R. B. KIMBER, Princeton, N.J.: Princeton University Press, 1970.

MEYER, HENRY C. *Mitteleuropa in German Thought, 1815–1945.* The Hague: Nijhoff, 1955.

MINDER, ROBERT. *Dichter in der Gesellschaft.* Frankfurt a./M.: Insel, 1966.

MOSSE, GEORGE L. *The Crisis of German Ideology: Intellectual Origins of the Third Reich.* New York: Grosset & Dunlap, 1964.

NATAN, ALEX (ed.). *German Men of Letters.* London: Wolff, 1961.

PASCAL, ROY. *The German Novel.* London: Methuen, 1965.

PENSA, MARIO. *Das Deutsche Denken.* Trans. from Italian by W. MECKAUER. Erlenbach-Zurich: Rentsch, 1948.

REHFISCH, HANS J. (ed.). *In Tyrannos: Four Centuries of Struggle Against Tyranny in Germany.* London: Drummond, 1944.

ROSE, ERNST. *A History of German Literature.* New York: New York University Press, 1960.

SELL, FRIEDRICH C. *Die Tragödie des Deutschen Liberalismus.* Stuttgart: Deutsche Verlags-Anstalt, 1953.

SILZ, WALTER. *Realism and Reality: Studies in the German Novelle of Poetic Realism.* Chapel Hill: University of North Carolina Press, 1954.

SNYDER, LOUIS L. *German Nationalism: The Tragedy of a People.* Harrisburg, Pa.: Stackpole Co., 1952.

Srbik, Heinrich Ritter von. *Geist und Geschichte vom Deutschen Humanismus bis zur Gegenwart,* 3rd ed. 2 vols. Munich and Salzburg: Müller, 1950.

Stern, Joseph P. *Re-Interpretations: Seven Studies in Nineteenth-Century German Literature.* New York: Basic Books, 1964.

Streisand, Joachim (ed.). *Studien über die Deutsche Geschichtswissenschaft,* 2nd rev. ed. 2 vols. Berlin: Akademie-Verlag, 1965.

Eighteenth-Century Background

Antoni, Carlo. *Der Kampf Wider die Vernunft.* Trans. from Italian by W. Goetz. Stuttgart: Koehler, 1951.

Bruford, Walter H. *Germany in the Eighteenth Century: The Social Background of the Literary Revival,* 2nd ed. Cambridge, England: The University Press, 1965.

Brüggemann, Fritz. *Der Kampf um die Bürgerliche Welt- und Lebensanschauung in der Deutschen Literatur des Achtzehnten Jahrhunderts.* Halle/Saale: Niemeyer, 1925.

Cassirer, Ernst. *The Philosophy of the Enlightenment.* Trans. by F. C. A. Koelln and J. P. Pettegrove. Boston: Beacon, 1964.

Dilthey, Wilhelm. *Das Erlebnis und die Dichtung.* Leipzig: Teubner, 1906.

Ermatinger, Emil. *Deutsche Kultur im Zeitalter der Aufklärung.* Potsdam: Akademische Verlagsgesellschaft, 1935.

Folkierski, Wladyslaw. *Entre le Classicisme et le Romantisme.* Paris: Champion, 1925.

Grappin, Pierre. *La Théorie du Génie dans le Préclassicisme Allemand.* Paris: Presses Universitaires de France, 1952.

Lúkacs, Georg. *Goethe and his Age.* Trans. by R. Anchor. London: Merlin, 1968.

Pascal, Roy. *The German Sturm und Drang.* New York: Philosophical Library, 1953.

Pinson, Koppel S. *Pietism as a Factor in the Rise of German Nationalism.* New York: Columbia University Press, 1934.

Ritter, Gerhard. *Frederick the Great.* Trans. by P. Paret. Berkeley and Los Angeles: University of California Press, 1968.

Rosenberg, Hans. *Bureaucracy, Aristocracy and Autocracy: The Prussian Experience, 1660–1815.* Cambridge, Mass.: Harvard University Press, 1958.

Small, Albion. *The Cameralists* (Chicago: University of Chicago Press, 1909).

Streisand, Joachim. *Geschichtliches Denken von der Deutschen Frühaufklärung bis zur Klassik,* 2nd rev. ed. Berlin: Akademie-Verlag, 1967.

Weil, Hans. *Die Entstehung des Deutschen Bildungsprinzips.* Bonn: Cohen, 1930.

Wolff, Hans. *Die Weltanschauung der Deutschen Aufklärung.* Munich: Lehnen, 1949.

From Revolution to Restoration: 1789–1815

Anderson, Eugene N. *Nationalism and the Cultural Crisis in Prussia, 1806–1815.* New York: Farrar and Rinehart, 1939.

Aris, Reinhold. *A History of Political Thought in Germany from 1789 to 1815.* London: Allen & Unwin, 1936.

BÉGUIN, ALBERT. L'Âme Romantique et le Rêve, 2nd ed. Paris: Corti, 1946.

———, (ed.). Le Romantisme Allemand: Textes et Études. Paris: Cahiers du Sud, 1949.

BRANDES, GEORG. Main Currents in Nineteenth-Century Literature. Trans. by D. WHITE and M. MORISON. (Vol. 2, The Romantic School.) London: Heinemann, 1923.

BRION, MARCEL. L'Allemagne Romantique. 2 vols. Paris: Michel, 1962.

———. Art of the Romantic Era. Trans. by D. CARROLL. London: Thames and Hudson, 1966.

BRUFORD, WALTER H. Culture and Society in Classical Weimar, 1775–1806. Cambridge, England: The University Press, 1962.

BRUNSCHWIG, HENRI. La Crise de l'État Prussien À La Fin du XVIIIᵉ Siècle et la Gènese de la Mentalité Romantique. Paris: Presses Universitaries de France, 1947.

DROZ, JACQUES. L'Allemagne et la Révolution Française. Paris: Presses Universitaires de France, 1949.

———. Le Romantisme Allemand et l'État. Paris: Payot, 1966.

EPSTEIN, KLAUS. The Genesis of German Conservatism, 1770–1806. Princeton, N.J.: Princeton University Press, 1966.

FORD, GUY S. Stein and the Era of Reform in Prussia, 1807–1815. Princeton, N.J.: Princeton University Press, 1922.

GODE-VON AESCH, ALEXANDER. Natural Science in German Romanticism. New York: Columbia University Press, 1941.

GOOCH, GEORGE P. Germany and the French Revolution. London: Longman's & Green, 1920.

JULKU, KYÖSTI. Die Revolutionäre Bewegung im Rheinland am Ende des Achtzehnter Jahrhunderts. 2 vols. Helsinki: Academia Scientiarum Fennica, 1969.

KELLY, GEORGE A. Idealism, Politics and History: Sources of Hegelian Thought. Cambridge, England: The University Press, 1969.

KOHN, LUDWIG W. Social Ideas in German Literature, 1770–1830. New York: Columbia University Press, 1938.

KORFF, HERMANN A. Geist der Goethezeit, 2nd ed. Leipzig: Hirzel, 1949.

———. Humanismus und Romantik. Leipzig: Weber, 1924.

LOVEJOY, ARTHUR O. Essays in the History of Ideas. New York: Capricorn, 1960.

MAYER, HANS. Zur Deutschen Klassik und Romantik. Stuttgart: Neske, 1963.

MEINECKE, FRIEDRICH. Das Zeitalter der Deutschen Erhebung, 1795–1815, 6th ed. Göttingen: Vandenhoeck & Ruprecht, 1957.

PECKHAM, MORSE. Beyond the Tragic Vision. New York: Braziller, 1962.

PESCH, LUDWIG. Die Romantische Rebellion in der Modernen Literatur und Kunst. Munich: Beck, 1962.

REGIN, DERIC. Freedom and Dignity: The Historical and Philosophical Thought of Schiller. The Hague: Nijhoff, 1965.

REHM, WALTHER. Griechentum und Goethezeit, 3rd ed. Munich: Lehnen, 1952.

REISS, HANS S. (ed.). Political Thought of the German Romantics, 1793–1815. Oxford: Blackwell, 1955.

SCHMITT, CARL. Politische Romantik. Munich and Leipzig: Duncker & Humboldt, 1919.

Silz, Walter. *Early German Romanticism.* Cambridge, Mass.: Harvard University Press, 1929.

Simon, Walter M. *The Failure of the Prussian Reform Movement, 1807–1819.* Ithaca: Cornell University Press, 1955.

Stahl, Ernst L. *Heinrich Von Kleist's Dramas,* rev. ed. Oxford: Blackwell, 1961.

Steinbüchel, Theodor (ed.). *Romantik, ein Zyklus Tübinger Vorlesungen.* Tübingen: Wunderlich, 1948.

Stern, Alfred. *Der Einfluss der Französischen Revolution auf das Deutsche Geistesleben.* Stuttgart and Berlin: Cotta, 1928.

Strich, Fritz. *Deutsche Klassik und Romantik,* 2nd rev. ed. Munich: Meyer & Jessen, 1924.

Tymms, Ralph. *German Romantic Literature.* London: Methuen, 1955.

Valjavec, Fritz. *Die Entstehung der Politischen Strömungen in Deutschland, 1770–1815.* Munich: Oldenbourg, 1951.

Walzel, Oskar. *German Romanticism.* Trans. by A. E. Lussky. New York: Putnam's, 1932.

Willoughby, Leonard A. *The Romantic Movement in Germany.* London: Oxford University Press, 1930.

Restoration and the Return of Revolution: 1815–1848

Brandes, Georg. *Main Currents in Nineteenth-Century Literature.* Trans. by D. White and M. Morison. (Vol. 6, *Young Germany*) London: Heinemann, 1923.

Butler, Eliza M. *The Saint-Simonian Religion in Germany.* Cambridge, England: The University Press, 1926.

Conze, Werner (ed.). *Staat und Gesellschaft im Deutschen Vormärz.* Stuttgart: Klett, 1962.

Droz, Jacques. *Europe Between Revolutions, 1815–1848.* Trans. by R. Baldick. New York: Harper & Row, 1967.

Engels, Friedrich. *Germany: Revolution and Counter-Revolution* in *The German Revolutions,* ed. by L. Krieger. Chicago: University of Chicago Press, 1967.

Fejtö, François (ed.). *The Opening of an Era, 1848.* London: Wingate, 1948.

Henderson, William O. *The Zollverein.* Cambridge, England: The University Press, 1939.

Hook, Sidney. *From Hegel to Marx,* 3rd ed. Ann Arbor: University of Michigan Press, 1968.

Legge, James G. *Rhyme and Revolution in Germany.* London: Constable, 1918.

McLellan, David. *The Young Hegelians and Karl Marx.* London: Macmillan, 1969.

Mannheim, Karl. *Essays on Sociology and Social Psychology,* ed. P. Kecskemeti. Oxford: The University Press, 1953.

Price, Arnold H. *The Evolution of the Zollverein.* Ann Arbor: University of Michigan Press, 1949.

Rohr, Donald G. *The Origins of Social Liberalism in Germany.* Chicago: University of Chicago Press, 1963.

Taylor, Ronald. *Hoffmann.* London: Bowes & Bowes, 1963.

THOMAS, RICHARD H. *Liberalism, Nationalism and the German Intellectuals, 1822–1847.* Cambridge, England. Heffner, 1951.

WEINBERG, KURT. *Henri Heine: "Romantique Defroqué."* Paris: Presses Universitaires de France, 1954.

Toward Unification and Consolidation: 1850–1890

BARZUN, JACQUES. *Darwin, Marx, Wagner,* rev. 2nd ed. Garden City, N.Y.: Doubleday, 1958.

DRU, ALEXANDER (ed.). *The Letters of Jacob Burckhardt.* New York: Pantheon, 1955.

EMERSON, RUPERT. *State and Sovereignty in Modern Germany.* New Haven: Yale University Press, 1928.

EYCK, ERICH. *Bismarck and the German Empire.* London: Allen & Unwin, 1958.

FRIEDJUNG, HEINRICH. *The Struggle for Supremacy in Germany, 1859–1866.* Trans. by A. J. P. TAYLOR and W. L. McELWEE. London: Macmillan, 1935.

HALLOWELL, JOHN H. *The Decline of Liberalism, with Particular Reference to German Politico–Legal Thought.* Berkeley and Los Angeles: University of California Press, 1943.

LEA, FRANK A. *The Tragic Philosopher: A Study of Friedrich Nietzsche.* London: Methuen, 1957.

MARTIN, ALFRED VON. *Burckhardt und Nietzsche,* 4th ed. Munich: Erasmus, 1947.

MARTINI, FRITZ. *Deutsche Literatur im Bürgerlichen Realismus, 1848–1898.* Stuttgart: Metzler, 1962.

MORGAN, GEORGE A. *What Nietzsche Means.* Cambridge, Mass.: Harvard University Press, 1941.

RAPHAEL, ROBERT. *Richard Wagner.* New York: Twayne, 1969.

ROSENBERG, ARTHUR. *Imperial Germany: The Birth of the German Republic, 1871–1918.* Trans. by I. F. D. MORROW, 2nd ed. Boston: Beacon, 1964.

SIMON, WALTER M. *Germany in the Age of Bismarck.* London: Allen & Unwin, 1968.

STERN, FRITZ. *The Politics of Cultural Despair: A Study in the Rise of the Germanic Ideology.* Garden City, N.Y.: Doubleday, 1965.

WANDREY, KONRAD. *Theodor Fontane.* Munich: Beck, 1919.

INDEX